A Song for the King

The mahāsiddha Saraha

A Song for the King

SARAHA ON MAHĀMUDRĀ MEDITATION

COMMENTARY
KHENCHEN THRANGU RINPOCHE

TRANSLATOR OF THE SONG AND EDITOR
MICHELE MARTIN

TRANSLATOR OF THE ORAL COMMENTARY
PETER O'HEARN

WISDOM PUBLICATIONS • BOSTON

Wisdom Publications, Inc.
199 Elm Street
Somerville MA 02144 USA
www.wisdompubs.org

Library of Congress Cataloging-in-Publication Data
Thrangu, Rinpoche, 1933-
  Song for the King : Saraha on mahamudra meditation / commentary, Khenchen
Thrangu Rinpoche ; translator of the Song and editor, Michele Martin ; translator
of the oral commentary, Peter O'Hearn.
     p. cm.
  Includes bibliographical references.
  ISBN 0-86171-503-9 (pbk. : alk. paper)
  1. Sarahapada, 8th cent. Dohakosa. 2. Religious life—Buddhism. 3. Mahamudra
(Tantric rite) I. Sarahapada, 8th cent. Dohakosa. English. II. Martin, Michele, 1942–
III. O'Hearn, Peter, 1959– IV. Title.
  BQ7775.S263T57 2006
  294.3'4435—dc22

                        2006000538

ISBN 0-86171-503-9

10 09 08 07 06
 5 4 3 2 1

Cover designed by Elizabeth Lawrence.
Back cover photo by Michele Martin: Thrangu Rinpoche on retreat at a Guru Rin-
poche cave in the Helambu region of Nepal's Himalayas.
Interior designed by Gopa & Ted2, Inc. Set in Adobe Garamond 11.25/16.8.
Frontispiece: The mahāsiddha Saraha; eastern Tibet, eighteenth century, opaque
watercolor on cotton. Detail from a tangka of four mahāsiddhas, © 2006 Museum
of Fine Arts, Boston.

♻ This book was produced with environmental mindfulness. We have elected to
print this title on 50% PCW recycled paper. As a result, we have saved the fol-
lowing resources: 17 trees, 786 lbs. of solid waste, 6,119 gallons of water, 1,474 lbs. of
greenhouse gases, and 12 million BTUs of energy. For more information, please visit
our web site, www.wisdompubs.org.

Contents

For the Seventeenth Gyalwang Karmapa,

Ogyen Trinley Dorjé

May his life be long and fruitful
May compassion like his unfold
in the hearts of every living being

Editor's Introduction

SARAHA HAS INSPIRED SEEKERS OF TRUTH for centuries with his spiritual songs and the legends of his life. Prominent among the eighty-four masters of India, he lived most probably in ninth-century Bengal.[1] Tradition holds that Saraha was the first to introduce mahāmudrā as the central practice of meditation,[2] and its relevance along with its lineage continue to the present day. On his visits to the West in the 1970s, the Sixteenth Karmapa, Rangjung Rigpé Dorjé, recommended mahāmudrā because it transcends all cultural barriers. The essence of Buddhist meditation is to tame our mind, and mahāmudrā practice does this through working directly with mind's nature, which is found to be the same in all living beings. Once this nature has been recognized, awareness of it is sustained in every situation, from meditation sessions to all facets of daily life. Over time, whatever arises is experienced as clear and fresh, beyond expression, and transparent to its radiant, empty nature.

Woven with analogies, spontaneous song is a natural medium for the expression of this ultimate reality. For this reality cannot be captured by a net of words and concepts but only indicated through the oblique lines of allusion. Metaphors have the capacity to evoke an experiential reality that transcends the intellect, and so they are not only a teaching tool to deepen understanding but an opening into another dimension. Saraha sang his songs to bring his listeners to enlightenment.

I

Thrangu Rinpoche's commentary belongs to the living oral tradition in which these verses began. Given in Colorado during the summer of 2002, his talks range from the basic points to the most subtle, all of which he has chosen for their relevance to meditation practice. The style of presentation reflects the oral tradition, which comes around to a topic from different directions, allowing this repetition to settle an idea more deeply into our minds. The tone is close to conversational, flowing in a timeless setting of spiritual friend and disciples. Thrangu Rinpoche based his explanations on a text by Karma Trinlépa (1456–1539), who has written the most extensive commentaries on Saraha's trilogy—his spiritual songs for the people, the queen, and the king.

A Song for the King is the shortest of the three compositions and the most profound, for it presents in greatest detail Saraha's unique interpretation of mahāmudrā. The eminent Kagyü scholar Pawo Tsuglak Trengwa (1504–66) wrote that the songs correspond to the three *kāyas,* or dimensions: *A Song for the People* relates to the nirmāṇakāya; *A Song for the Queen* relates to the sambhogakāya, and, finally, *A Song for the King* relates to the dharmakāya, which makes it the most subtle and succinct.[3]

In their Indian form, songs of realization were presented in a flow of verses without an overt structure. It was the Tibetan commentaries that added the outlines and gave a topography to the landscape the songs explored. In particular, Karma Trinlépa's outline is quite detailed and could actually serve as a summary of his whole commentary.

To introduce the song, let us look at an overview. At the beginning, Karma Trinlépa uses the occasion of the traditional homage to elucidate four major obstacles to practice. This discussion functions as the traditional preliminaries for a text or practice. Following this, he presents the usual précis of a text, which alerts the reader to the range of its content, by dividing the verses into a summary of mahāmudrā, according to ground, path, and fruition. He then returns to each one of these for an extensive discussion as he builds the rest of his commentary.

In the longer presentation, Saraha's verses on the ground start with his advice to keep it clear of attachment, especially to the various signs of accomplishment that might arise from practice. This is a theme that runs throughout the song, as these attachments are the basic way that we deviate from an authentic path. In all the major manuals on mahāmudrā, instructions on how to practice are followed by descriptions of how to avoid obstacles—all the diversions and sidetracks that lead us astray. Saraha distributes these cautions liberally throughout his song.

After warning us of dangers, Saraha defines classic concepts, such as the nonduality of appearance and emptiness, and then he points out the essential nature of mind. When we are meditating, it is important to know what we are seeking, for this goal will guide the whole process of practice. Therefore, in the beginning Saraha points to ultimate reality, the fruition that is the realization of mind's very nature. Finally, he speaks about cause and effect, which constitute the level of relative truth, and about the perils of fixating on scholastic analysis.

Having provided this ground, Saraha begins his mapping of the path with another series of verses on the dangers of attachment, in particular the peril of taking meditative experience to be something real and truly existent. Once this is complete, Saraha sets forth the actual path through his unique presentation of mahāmudrā, laid out as the four symbols or stages of practice: (1) mindfulness, (2) nonminding, (3) the unborn, and (4) beyond the intellect.

In his commentary on *A Song for the People*, Karma Trinlépa gives a detailed explanation of these four stages in increasingly subtle levels.[4] Since the third and secret one has been emphasized by Thrangu Rinpoche and prefigures the discussion in this book, it might be useful to look at it briefly. In *A Song for the People*, Saraha's verse reads:

...the four stages: mindfulness, nonminding, the unborn, and
    beyond the intellect. Among these, I first teach *mindfulness.*
As you drink the elixir of *nonminding,* apprehending "I" and
    "mine" is forgotten.
Whoever realizes that mind itself is forever unborn will come to
    know the reality of the single letter *A, the unborn.*
Ultimately *beyond the intellect,* the nature of mind knows neither
    name nor symbol.[5]

Karma Trinlépa explains that this verse indicates how to realize mind's
abiding nature to be "uncontaminated," which means free of mental
pollution, or "beyond the intellect," the final of the four stages. The
three stages leading up to this begin with *mindfulness,* which Karma
Trinlépa defines as a practice that cuts through the root of the mind.
What this might mean is described by another master:

Cutting through elaborations from without or from within—
There is not only one, but many ways to teach the view.
Nevertheless, just as dousing a fire naturally stops its smoke,
It is more profound to cut through the roots of your mind from
    within.[6]

Here, the cutting through of mindfulness means to calm the busyness of
proliferating concepts. This reins in a distracted, overactive mind and
brings it into a more tranquil state.

    The next stage, *nonminding,* is an extension of the first. Karma Trin-
lépa writes that to rest in a state free of mental activity is to drink the
elixir of nonminding; this induces an experience in which the concepts
that grasp onto "I" and "mine" slip from our mind. Since apprehending
an "I"—the actual basis for the afflictions—is no longer present, Saraha
states that the mind is "completely purified of all afflictions." Thus freed,

we are no longer depressed by faults or inflated by positive qualities. The ups and downs of that rollercoaster ride have ended. (Appendix 4, "Some Reflections on *Dran med*," gives an extended discussion of non-minding.)

Through abiding in this second stage, we come to the third, the *unborn*. With the aid of the key instructions, we realize a deeper reality—the unborn emptiness that the letter *A* embodies. This is seeing that the mind itself is forever unborn and that this quality is all-pervasive; it is the very nature of our mind and of all phenomena. Karma Trinlépa states that with the realization of this unborn nature, samsara is transcended.

Ultimately we arrive at the fourth stage, *beyond the intellect*. Karma Trinlépa explains that through the oral instructions we have practiced in the past, we have come to a realization that transcends even the name or symbol of the unborn: all these are liberated into a state beyond expression in thought or word.[7]

These four stages of Saraha bear a close resemblance to the famous four yogas of mahāmudrā, which also chart a path to full awakening.[8] Since they resonate so clearly with one another, let us look briefly at how they interrelate and illuminate each other.

The first yoga of *one-pointedness* has a quality of tranquility like Saraha's first stage of mindfulness, in which discursiveness is brought to rest. During the second yoga, *free of elaborations,* or *simplicity,* all experience dissolves into emptiness without leaving a trace. This resembles the second stage of nonminding when highs and lows no longer disturb our mind. During the third yoga of *one taste,* we realize that all phenomena are appearance and emptiness inseparable. In Saraha's third stage of the unborn, we realize that our mind and all phenomena have the same nature, or embody the same taste. Everything is unborn. With the fourth yoga, *nonmeditation,* spontaneous presence is reached, and all subtle dualistic appearances utterly dissolve. This is also Saraha's fourth stage, completely beyond the intellect; it is the ultimate that transcends expression.

After laying out these four stages, Saraha puts the final touches on his map of the journey to full awakening with another reminder of nonattachment and clear advice on how to meditate: Realize that there is nothing to negate, nothing to affirm, and nothing to be meditated upon. Since mere recognition brings liberation, we simply continue, "recognizing what is clear and unmoving." This will lead to the fruition of full awakening: Mind expands into vast wisdom, the five kāyas appear, and benefits continually flow forth as the mind remains flawless and unobstructed. Saraha concludes his verses with a vision of ultimate reality fully integrated and fully functioning within our relative world.

*   *   *   *

This version of *A Song for the King* has been created with a varied readership in mind. For the growing number of people who know Tibetan, the original text is reproduced. In an appendix, a scholarly translation is provided with Karma Trinlépa's detailed outline and interpolations from his commentary marked in brackets. This layout will also help those who wish to work directly with the text in a traditional manner by reciting and memorizing the verses. In the main body of the text with the verses accompanying Thrangu Rinpoche's commentary, the brackets have been removed for smoother reading, and the outline has been condensed to reflect the essential and Thrangu Rinpoche's emphasis.

Nothing happens without the cooperation of many people, and I am grateful for their kind and generous assistance. David Germano found, copied, and sent the Tibetan manuscript of Karma Trinlépa's commentary by courier to Kathmandu. Through the Tibetan Buddhist Resource Center, E. Gene Smith provided a copy of the root text. Peter O'Hearn gave his usual precise and eloquent oral translation and was wonderful to work with during the editing process. Cathy Jackson transcribed the

EDITOR'S INTRODUCTION   7

talks, Clark Johnson worked on early stages of the text, and the final polish was given by Tracy Davis. Pema Tsewang Shastri input the Tibetan root text and David Kittelstrom at Wisdom Publications has offered superb support throughout. In addtion to editing the commentary, I am responsible for the translation of the song and outline, the notes, glossary, and appendixes. At my doorstep as well sits whatever is mistaken, rough, or unclear.

It is my hope that this book will inspire readers to practice mahā-mudrā and that it will bring them great benefit all along the way to perfect and full awakening.

Michele Martin

Approaching Mahāmudrā   1

ŚĀKYAMUNI BUDDHA taught in eighty-four thousand different ways. The authentic practice of any one of these teachings leads to liberation and omniscience in the long term, and in the short term it pacifies difficult situations, calms our minds, and fosters insight. Among all the teachings of the Buddha, from the early time of the Kagyü lineage masters up to the present day, mahāmudrā has been selected as the principal teaching of the lineage. Due to its prominence, there are unusually profound instructions concerning this practice, which was considered the most beneficial.

Mahāmudrā is also the easiest aspect of the teachings to implement, and its practice has produced a great number of realized masters. Especially now, with the flourishing of Buddhism in the West, mahāmudrā is an even more appropriate practice than it was in the past. I have found that many Westerners practice Dharma out of great interest and devotion, and I feel that the only aspect of Dharma that will actually satisfy their hopes and aspirations is mahāmudrā, because it opens a direct path to realizing mind's nature and can be practiced in conjunction with any activity.

When people practice Dharma, their individual circumstances greatly affect what they can and will do. Some people are able to practice with great intensity and great diligence in long retreats. Others with the same degree of faith and interest may lack the opportunity for such intense and prolonged practice. In teaching Dharma, we must fulfill the needs and hopes of both types of practitioner. Some people possess the resources and circumstances that allow them to become monastics and devote their lives to practice. Some people possess the resources that allow them to practice in long, intense retreats. But all of these practitioners without exception are devoted to Dharma, and so they should have a system that equally enables and benefits their different kinds of Dharma practice. That system is mahāmudrā, and there is none better for all types of practitioners.

An effective practice of mahāmudrā requires access to genuine texts of Dharma instruction. For over a thousand years, the uncommon, practical instructions of the Kagyü lineage have existed in Tibetan, but until recently the barrier of language has come between Western students and mahāmudrā instructions. Now, through the diligent effort of Western students, major texts from the lineage have been translated and made available.[9] These texts are eminently practical and not cryptic or inaccessible. They provide appropriate solutions and responses to the various types of experiences, both positive and negative, that might appear in our practice. With these new translations, we now have the necessary resources for understanding mahāmudrā practice.

Saraha's *Song for the King* belongs to the lineage of mahāmudrā instruction, which comes to us in two ways: through a long lineage and a short one. The short or close lineage, which is better known, begins with the dharmakāya Vajradhara and passes on to Tilopa, Nāropa, Marpa, and others.[10] The long lineage, which is found in many lineage supplications, also begins with Vajradhara and then goes to the bodhisattva Ratnamati, the mahāsiddha Saraha, Nāgārjuna, and others, eventually down to Marpa.[11] Saraha is an important link in this long lineage of mahāmudrā instructions, which continues unbroken down to the present day.

Many of the compositions of the Indian mahāsiddhas have been scattered because they are separate, short texts, and therefore many have been lost. But due to the kindness of the Seventh Gyalwang Karmapa, Chödrak Gyatso, the Indian sources for the mahāmudrā teachings have been preserved. He collected all of these compositions into three volumes, which he titled *Indian Sources of Mahāmudrā*. They include the Buddha's original mahāmudrā teachings, found in the tantras, plus the oral instructions and spiritual songs composed by the mahāsiddhas, such as this one by Saraha. Because of Chödrak Gyatso, the lineage of reading transmissions and explanations of mahāmudrā has not disappeared, and now there is no danger of them being lost in the future. His Holiness the Sixteenth Karmapa, Rangjung Rigpé Dorjé, bestowed the reading transmission of these three volumes at Rumtek Monastery, and I had the good fortune to receive this transmission in its entirety.

The Life of Saraha

Saraha was born into the Brahmin caste and became a Buddhist monastic named Rāhulabhadra. He was a very influential and highly respected teacher of Buddhism within the monastic tradition, enjoying the patronage, devotion, and faith of a king and his subjects. Then one day, while still engaged in teaching and practice, Saraha encountered a wisdom ḍākinī who appeared in the form of a woman from a very low caste. At that time in India, social class and caste were considered of great importance. This woman was an arrow maker, and Saraha encountered her at a crossroads where she was making arrows.

When Saraha saw this woman putting the feathers on an arrow, he noticed that she was doing it in a way that was extremely concentrated, not looking to the right or left but one-pointedly working on the arrow. The shaft had three segments and Saraha watched her cut off the base as well as the tip and split the base into four, where she tied a pebble in place. At the tip she placed the arrowhead and at the base she placed four feathers. Saraha addressed her, saying, "Are you making an arrow?" In reply she said, "Son of noble family, the realizations of all buddhas are understood through skillful methods and indications, not through words and writing."

It dawned on Saraha that she must be a ḍākinī and that what she said was a symbolic indication for him to understand. This is what he understood. The three segments of the shaft symbolized the three kāyas of the dharmakāya, sambhogakāya, and nirmāṇakāya. Cutting off the root symbolized cutting off cyclic existence at its very origin, and cutting off the tip of the shaft symbolized the severing of ego-clinging.

Furthermore, he understood that placing the arrowhead onto the shaft symbolized wisdom and that dividing the base into four symbolized the four aspects of mahāmudrā practice: mindfulness, nonminding, the unborn, and beyond the intellect.[12] Placing the pebble into these four splits and tying it with a string symbolized unifying method and wisdom (Skt. *upāya* and *prajñā*) through the practice of calm abiding and deeper insight (Skt. *śamatha* and *vipaśyanā*). Inserting the four feathers symbolized the four aspects of view, meditation, conduct, and fruition.

Saraha understood the straightening of the arrow as following the straight path from the very beginning. The woman closed one eye and opened the other while checking the straightness of the arrow. This symbolized closing the eye of dualistic mind while opening the eye of wisdom. At the moment when Saraha fully realized the state of mahāmudrā, he exclaimed "*da.*" This is a play on the sound of this word, which can mean either "arrow" or "symbol."[13] He said, "You are not an arrow maker. You are a symbol maker." From that point onward Saraha changed his lifestyle from that of a monk to that of a siddha.

He began to travel around with her and practice the Dharma. By living with her rather than being a celibate monk, Saraha greatly disappointed the king and his subjects. So to convince Saraha to return to a more conventional monastic lifestyle, the king sent a group of his subjects to ask Saraha to behave properly. Saraha's response to their request was what is known as *A Song for the People,* which is the first of the three great spiritual songs, or *dohas,* sung by Saraha in the vernacular of southern India. *A Song for the People* is the longest of the three songs, comprising one hundred sixty verses of instruction in mahāmudrā. Through hearing Saraha's teaching, the people sent by the king all developed great realization and stopped asking Saraha to behave. When they returned to the court, the king observed that they had been unsuccessful, so he decided to send a second deputation, which was made up of the queen and her retinue of servants. They too asked Saraha to behave, and his response was the second spiritual song, *A Song for the Queen,* in eighty verses. In response to this teaching, the queen and her retinue, like the people before, attained authentic realization, stopped pestering Saraha, and returned to the court. Observing that both the people and the queen had been unsuccessful, the king decided to go personally and ask Saraha to mend his ways. Saraha's response to the king's petition was *A Song for the King.* It consists of forty stanzas, and upon hearing it, the king immediately attained supreme siddhi, or full awakening.

A Song for the King

The literature of mahāmudrā consists of Indian spiritual songs, such as the *Three Spiritual Songs* of Saraha, the *Ganges Mahāmudrā* of Tilopa, and many similar songs of realization by Tibet's great masters, such as Marpa and Milarepa. There are also Tibetan commentaries on mahāmudrā, among them *The Ocean of Definitive Meaning* by the Ninth Karmapa, Wangchuk Dorjé. The commentaries and spiritual songs reflect the same outlook, present essentially the same material, and have the same meaning. But these two sources of mahāmudrā are quite different in how they present their subject. The commentaries give a systematic and clear presentation of mahāmudrā instructions from the very beginning of the path up to its end. By contrast, the spiritual songs are not systematic and sequential, as they are usually sung when a mahāsiddha develops realization and spontaneously expresses that realization through the bliss of the realization itself. Spiritual songs are more an expression of personal realization than a systematic presentation of the path. For example, in *The Ocean of Definitive Meaning* you will find a gradual presentation starting with how to practice tranquility meditation and then, upon mastering this, how to practice insight meditation, and so on. Usually spiritual songs do not present the path in such a sequential manner. Therefore, in studying the spiritual songs, which are both poetic and cryptic, we need the support of the great texts of instruction, even though the essential meaning of all of the instruction is still found in the songs themselves. The one I am using is *The Middle-Length Commentary on "A Song for the King"* by Karma Trinlépa,[14] who was the teacher of the Eighth Gyalwang Karmapa, Mikyö Dorjé. Karma Trinlépa wrote commentaries on all three of Saraha's spiritual songs.

In *A Song for the King*, mahāmudrā is taught in three aspects: ground, path, and fruition. This spiritual song answers the questions: What is the ground or basis of mahāmudrā practice? What is the path or process of this practice? What is the result or goal of this practice? In this song, the ground is how things really are.[15] From this perspective, the way that we experience ordinary appearances is confused. These mundane or samsaric appearances refer to how things appear. But what are they really? How are things in their abiding or true nature? In other words, what lies behind the confused appearances of phenomena? It must be this true nature, recognized as the very excellence of this ground, which makes the path of mahāmudrā possible. So the first subject of our text is an explanation of the foundation of mahāmudrā—what is to be realized, or how things really are. The path to realizing mahāmudrā is path mahāmudrā. And finally, the culmination of that path is fruition mahāmudrā, the state of full realization. *A Song for the King* is structured along these lines of ground, path, and fruition. In the beginning, it gives a brief presentation of all three aspects, and then they are presented extensively using numerous analogies.

The Meaning of Mahāmudrā

The Sanskrit term mahāmudrā was translated by mahāsiddhas and great translators into Tibetan as *chag gya chen po*.[16] Looking at the literal meaning of the Tibetan translation can be useful in understanding what mahāmudrā is all about. When a symbolic etymology[17] or explanation of *chag gya chen po* is given, it is said that *chag* represents great emptiness, and *gya* represents nondual wisdom. On first glance, this is somewhat cryptic, because there is no obvious connection between the Tibetan word *chag* and emptiness, nor between the Tibetan word *gya* and nondual wisdom. In common usage, the word *chag* is an honorific term for someone's hand, and the term *gya* means either "vast" as an adjective or "seal" as a noun. However, if we look at the word *chag* carefully, the first thing we see is that this word is used a lot in Tibetan. For example, the word for "salutation" or "prostration" is *chag tsal wa*.[18] When we speak of the Buddha's hand, we use the honorific word *chag* rather than the ordinary word *lag pa*. The honorific is used for anyone else whom we esteem, such as teachers, monarchs, and ministers. Nevertheless, the word *chag* has another usage. When it is not used as an honorific for hand, it has the connotation of "clean" or "cleansing." For example, a broom is also called a *chag ma*,[19] which literally means a cleanser. The reason *chag*, which has the connotation of cleansing, is the honorific form for hand is that whatever comes from the hand of buddhas or mahāsiddhas, such as their writings and their actions, has the primary function of cleansing, purifying, or removing the misery and obscurations of living beings. Returning to the idea of great emptiness, it is now possible to see a connection between the word *chag* and the state of emptiness. All things are empty in their nature. Not recognizing this, we suffer and experience samsara. If this emptiness is recognized, that very recognition cleanses or removes all suffering. It is emptiness and the recognition of emptiness that cleanses us of suffering. In sum, the deeper explanation for the word *chag* is "great emptiness," which purifies our suffering.

The second syllable *gya* usually means either "that which is vast" or "a seal." The connection between the idea of a seal and the idea of vastness is that of an imprint. For example, a handprint not only depicts the hand, but it also shows the extent of the hand. So the extent or imprint of something shows what that thing fills or pervades. The second syllable, therefore, points out the fact that while emptiness is indeed the nature of all phenomena, emptiness is not a voidness: it is simultaneously nondual wisdom. In other words, emptiness itself has an innate aspect of lucidity.[20] The second syllable indicates that emptiness is an expanse of wisdom, or one could say, emptiness is pervaded with wisdom. Finally, the third word is the two syllables of *chen po,* which means "great." It points to the understanding that this expanse of wisdom, which is emptiness, is great in being all-pervasive.

In this way, it is quite clear that mahāmudrā is concerned with meditation on emptiness as taught by the Buddha. But when we use the term *emptiness,* we may understand it in different ways. We may see emptiness as something positive or as something negative—an absence of experience and thought, an utter lack of qualities, or a state of absolute nothingness. That, however, is not what emptiness is, because it also contains an inherent lucidity. Since emptiness is at the same time great wisdom, it is the root of all that is beneficial. One could say that this emptiness is the potential and source of all wisdom that knows the true nature of phenomena. Therefore, while the nature to be realized is emptiness, that nature itself possesses inherent lucidity or wisdom. The instructions for realizing this true nature, including its inherent wisdom, constitute what we call mahāmudrā.

The Song Begins   2

OW WE TURN to Saraha's song, which is explained in the tradi-
tional manner, beginning with the title and the homage of the
translator.

> In the Indian language, the title is: *Doha Kosha Nama Charya Giti.*
> In Tibetan, it is: *Doha mdzod ces bya ba spyod pa'i glu.* In English:
> *From the Treasury of Spiritual Songs, A Song of Yogic Conduct.*

The title "A Song for the King" was added by the Tibetan translators fol-
lowing the narrative of how the three songs arose. The first was "A Song
for the People," the second, "A Song for the Queen," and the third, "A
Song for the King." The word *doha* can be translated as "song of attain-
ment" or "song of experience."[21]

> I prostrate to Noble Mañjuśrī.[22]

"Noble" also means "elevated," indicating that he is far above ordinary
individuals and abides on a pure bodhisattva level.

The Homage to the Deity by Saraha

I prostrate to the one who has vanquished the power of the māras.

This homage is the first part of the song that was actually composed by Saraha. "The one who has vanquished the power of the māras" can be understood as referring to mahāmudrā itself, which has the power to conquer or remove the māras. In colloquial language, the term *māras* refers to external demons that try to tempt one in various ways. But according to the Buddhist tradition, *māra* in its fundamental sense refers to a factor that brings about suffering for oneself and others; in other words, it is anything that causes unhappiness and suffering. There are four types of māras. The first is called *kleśa-māra,* which means the "māra of afflictions." We have within us three major afflictions, or disturbing emotions: ignorance, attachment, and aversion. The five afflictions are these three plus jealousy and greed. They all create a great deal of suffering, for when they are present in a person, they can cause further suffering in others. They are the root of everything that keeps us in samsara, and therefore these disturbing emotions need to be conquered. It is the practice of mahāmudrā that is the best way to achieve liberation from samsara.

We also possess the five aggregates of form, sensation, perception, formation, and consciousness. These constitute the second māra, the *skandha-māra,* or the māra of the aggregates. Because they are composite, the aggregates change and fall apart, and in this shifting and disintegration, they form an intrinsic part of samsara's cycle. For example, at the end of the twelve links of interdependent origination, which trace how samsara arises and ceases, it is said that from birth comes aging and death. From that come suffering, lamenting, and all manner of misery. In short, the aggregates are the proximate condition for the arising of suffering. Their falling apart and changing lead directly to suffering; therefore, to go beyond suffering, we must transcend them.

THE SONG BEGINS 19

The third māra is called *mṛtyupati-māra,* or the Lord of Death, who is depicted as a wrathful and terrifying demon representing death itself, the end of a given life. It is also is something we need to move beyond in the sense of not being prey to the fear of death. If we practice meditation on mahāmudrā and realize the nature of our mind, we will have control over our rebirth and will not fear death. It is mahāmudrā that finally conquers the Lord of Death.

These three māras are also depicted iconographically. The māra of the afflictions is presented as a Brahmin. The māra of the aggregates is depicted as someone afflicted with extreme old age and infirmity. The māra of the Lord of Death is depicted as the terrifying demon of death, Yamantaka. The practice of Dharma frees us from these three māras.

The fourth māra is what obstructs the practice of Dharma and prevents us from becoming free of these first three māras. It is called *deva-putra-māra,* or the māra of the child of the gods. A child of the gods sounds delightful, and this māra is depicted as a very attractive person wearing beautiful jewelry and clothing. It is actually all desirable things—what is pleasing to the eye, ear, nose, tongue, and touch. But their attractiveness is not the problem; it is our craving for and fixation on these pleasures and desirable states that prevents us from conquering the other three māras.

To summarize, there are four māras to be conquered or transcended. In moving beyond them, we achieve liberation from samsara and the full manifestation of our spontaneously present wisdom. Here, in the author's homage, mahāmudrā is praised because it conquers all four māras and thereby brings about liberation and omniscience.

A Brief Presentation of Ground Mahāmudrā

A Song for the King is divided into the ground, path, and fruition of mahāmudrā. In the beginning, these three aspects of mahāmudrā are presented very concisely; in later verses, they are presented extensively. This section encompasses the first brief presentation of ground, path, and fruition. We begin with ground mahāmudrā, which has three sections: abandoning attachment, developing positive qualities, and understanding what to take up and what to reject.

Ultimate truth—the true nature of things, or dharmatā—never changes. Within it, there is no change or fluctuation, and this is referred to as emptiness. It is for this reason the *Heart Sutra* states that there is no form, no sound, no smell, and so forth.[23] Emptiness is the nature of the ground itself, but we do not experience things as being empty. We experience objects, such as trees or people, in the way they appear to us, as more or less solid things. Therefore, we may doubt that all phenomena are empty. If the nature of things is emptiness, then why are there appearances? The answer to this question is dealt with in the next section of the song.

In his *Song of the Self-Arisen Nature,* the first Jamgön Kongtrül Lodrö Tayé also gives an explanation of the ground, path, and fruition of mahāmudrā.[24] He explains that ground mahāmudrā has to do with the nature of things and with how we confuse phenomena. This means there are two aspects to an explanation of ground mahāmudrā: the way things actually are and the way in which confusion arises. What we need to realize in our meditation is how things really are, the true nature of phenomena. At present, we do not experience phenomena as they really are but know them in a confused or incorrect manner. While the nature of everything is emptiness, we do not experience things as empty but as various rather solid appearances. So we need to understand what these misperceptions are and how they arise.

The first three verses give the brief presentation of ground mahāmudrā. What do we mean by *ground?* We wish to achieve liberation from suffering and the bewildered appearances of samsara, and the reason we can free ourselves is due to the fact that these phenomena are temporary or adventitious appearances coming from our confusion.²⁵ Another way to say this is that they do not truly exist as they appear. If we understand this, then we understand something about the foundation of liberation, which is ground mahāmudrā. From that point of view, the path of mahāmudrā is the process of eradicating bewilderment and bewildered appearances. When all bewilderment or confusion has been eliminated and, thereby, all the innate qualities of the ground are revealed, we have reached fruition mahāmudrā.

How Delusive Appearances Arise within the Ground

1.   Just as when the wind blows
      And still water is turned into moving waves,
      So the appearing Saraha is just one,
      Yet the king creates diverse appearances.

The first verse of the song concerns the confused way we perceive phenomena, which is presented through an analogy of water and waves: "Just as when the wind blows and still water is turned into moving waves...." There is no substantial difference between water and the waves that arise on its surface; the waves have no existence separate from the water itself. Nevertheless, with the presence of the wind, waves appear as distinct entities or manifestations of the water. In the same way, due to the presence of confusion (the wind), appearances (the waves) arise in our experience. These projections of our bewilderment are nonexistent appearances; they are of themselves nothing other than the manifestation of our confusion. The meaning of this analogy can be applied to all phenomena and in particular to the mind, which is, after all, the principal focus of mahāmudrā. It is within the mind that the resolution of the nature of things is gained. The mind itself, however, has no form, color, shape, or any other substantial characteristic, and yet thoughts continuously arise. These thoughts that appear within the mind have no existence apart from the mind. They partake of no nature other than that of the mind itself, and yet they appear as distinct objects or events.

The point of this analogy of water and waves is to explain how phenomena appear within the dharmadhātu (the expanse of all phenomena), which is another name for the nature of the mind. From the perspective of mind itself, the analogy explains how thoughts arise as the display of mind's own nature. From the perspective of phenomena in general, the analogy shows how the nature of phenomena arises as the appearance of various things.

The second two lines of the first verse employ a different analogy, related to the immediate situation in which Saraha is singing the song. In response to the presence and petition of the king, Saraha observes, "So the appearing Saraha is just one, yet the king creates diverse appearances." This means that while Saraha remains one person, the king has diverse perceptions of him. When he thinks about Saraha's caste, he perceives Saraha as a Brahmin. Sometimes he sees him as a great paṇḍita, because Saraha was an eminent Buddhist scholar. Sometimes he sees Saraha as a monastic, because Saraha had received monastic ordination. Finally, since Saraha had broken caste and monastic codes by consorting with the arrow maker, he also sees Saraha as a degenerate yogi. But in fact, there is only one Saraha. It is the king's perception, or his projection, that sees all of these manifestations of Saraha as distinct persons. In the same way, while there are no distinctions within the expanse of the dharmadhātu, we nevertheless perceive a variety of phenomena. So through two analogies, this first verse on the ground of mahāmudrā shows that confused projections come about: while the ground of appearances is emptiness, within that ground bewildered appearances arise.

How Subject and Object Appear to Be Separate

2.   The ignorant press their eyes[26]
       And see one lamp as two.
       Like this, in mind's nature where seer and seen are not two,
       Alas! The mind appears as two things.

The first verse showed the presence of our confusion, and this second verse specifies how this confusion comes about. Confusion, or false view, arises because we perceive things in a dual way that brings up the perceived object and the perceiving subject. We have an incorrect belief in the dualism that posits an object of experience and a subject that experiences it. Bewilderment, therefore, is not just mere bewilderment; it is double bewilderment because neither subject nor object ultimately exists. Take the example of an experience of the senses. When you see something, you assume that the external object exists as an object and that it also exists as a subjective thought, or perception, within the mind. We experience the mind as an experiencing mental conscious-ness, and we experience objects as being within the mind and able to be experienced. However, the objects of mental consciousness are gen-eralized abstractions,[27] resemblances of actual sense experience. They arise as generic images within the mind and are accompanied by lin-guistic abstractions.[28] These are mistakenly perceived as being inher-ently linked to the objects to which they refer. In fact, the object of experience has no inherent connection to the linguistic label that the mind applies to it.

The falseness of believing in the existence of subject and object is explained in this second verse, which presents the situation of seeing something double, because we are rolling our eyes back or pressing on them. If we squeeze our eyes and look at a lamp, we will see two lamps. We cannot say that we do not see two lamps, because we actually do see two lamps. At the same time, we know there are not really two lamps there. The dual lamps are an optical illusion created by our pressing on our eyes. In the same way, when we experience phenomena, even though there is no subject and no object, because of our ignorance (the pressure on our eyes), our experience is divided into two.

Seeing two lamps instead of one is an analogy for what we do when we divide our mind into the one that perceives things and the apparent external things. In its true nature, the mind is not divisible into subject and object, just as there are not two lamps when the eyes are pressed. It is because we perceive the mind as divided into subject and object that we perceive incorrectly. So Saraha says, "Alas!" It is a shame that we see things in a way they are not.

The first verse showed that while the nature of all phenomena is emptiness, through our ignorance, the whole variety of phenomena arise just as waves arise in a body of water. With the analogy of the two lamps, the second verse explains how this incorrect belief arises through the dualistic perception of subject and object. Taken together, these first two stanzas describe the nature of confusion as seeing what does not exist.

The nature of all perceived phenomena is emptiness, utter peace and perfection. This emptiness is also lucidity and the space for the unlimited possibility of manifestation. It is the nature of the perceiving mind, yet we do not normally see it. Our ignorance has two aspects: We do not see what actually exists (emptiness), and we see what does not really exist (the duality).

This empty nature of the mind and phenomena is not, however, a voidness because it is pervaded by wisdom. Due to its lucidity, emptiness has the inherent capacity to manifest appearances. We might then ask, Why do we not see this nature of emptiness as it really is? The first two verses answer this question by demonstrating how we see what is not there. The third verse is concerned with how we do not see what is there.

Primordial Wisdom Pervades the World

3.   Though many lamps are lit throughout the house,
      Those with no eyes to see remain in darkness.
      Like this, though spontaneous wisdom is all-pervasive and nearby,
      For the ignorant it is far, far away.

The third stanza presents the analogy of a sightless person in a well-illuminated place. If we were to light many lamps in a room that was dark, anyone who could see would be able to perceive things in the room. But if someone were sightless, the illumination of the lamps would have no effect and the person would continue to see nothing. This is an analogy for the way ignorance prevents us from seeing things as they are.

The fundamental nature, found within each and every being, is spontaneously present wisdom. This wisdom is "all-pervasive and nearby." It is all-pervasive because it is present within every being without exception. It is nearby because it is our own nature, not distant or inaccessible to us. This wisdom, also called the sugatagarbha or buddha nature, is definitely within us, but we do not detect it because ignorance has obscured our seeing of it. And so, in thinking about our buddha nature, we tend to conceive of it as something very difficult to obtain and far away, even though it is our own nature.

This ignorance in not recognizing our own nature is the source of all our problems and our suffering. To realize our own nature is the fruition of the path, the attainment of buddhahood. To make clear what this result is, it might be helpful to look at the Tibetan word for the Buddha, which is *sang gye*. The first syllable, *sang*, means "to cleanse or remove" and refers to the removal of ignorance. What is meant by the removal of ignorance? Imagine that you are dreaming and in your dream you drive somewhere, get into a bad accident, and are seriously injured. What do you really need to get rid of this pain and suffering? No amount of medical treatment or vehicle repair will actually help this situation, because the whole time you are safely asleep in your bed. The only remedy that will actually get rid of your suffering is the recognition that you are just dreaming and no accident has occurred. As soon as you realize this, your suffering will disappear. This example illustrates that the elimination of our ignorance is simply removal, or *sang*.

The second syllable, *gye,* means "expanded" or "blossomed." When ignorance is removed, appearances caused by it cease, and, consequently, there is no fear. There is no need to do anything, because our innate wisdom, which was always there, is simply and fully revealed. This revelation of our innate wisdom is what *gye*, or blossomed, refers to. Attaining the fruition of the path does not involve going somewhere we have never been or receiving something from someone else. Fruition is nothing other than the recognition of our own true nature. If we wake from sleep, the dream will dissolve and we will experience the relief of being safe in the bed of our true nature.

The method through which we achieve this awakening is called the three vehicles of Buddhist practice. We could define these three vehicles as the simple explanation, the more profound explanation, and the profoundest explanation. The first vehicle is the Foundational Vehicle, which explains how the cause of our suffering is the accumulation of karma, motivated by the disturbing emotions. If we wish to end our negative karma, we need to eliminate the disturbing emotions. According to the Foundational Vehicle, these begin with the false perception of self and other. When we believe in these, we begin to believe in a self. By fixating on it, all our disturbing emotions arise.

We may, for example, develop an attachment to anything that gratifies the self and develop an aversion toward anything that is unpleasant or that threatens the self. This attachment leads straight into the disturbing emotions of desire and aggression. Unfortunately, we cannot give up fixation on a self simply by thinking, "Now I will give up this fixation." The only way to give it up is to recognize the nature of the ground, which is the nonexistence of the self. In mahāmudrā, we do this through a technique called *looking for the self*. We ask, What is my body? Where is my body? and so forth. Through questioning, we discover that this "I" that seems so solid and real, like something that endures from birth to death, has actually never existed. When we finally recognize the nonexistence of the self, our fixation on it naturally vanishes and thereby our suffering also ends. In sum, the principal object of meditation in the Foundational Vehicle is the meditation on the selflessness of persons, and through it, the fruition of this vehicle is achieved.

In the second vehicle, the Mahayana or Greater Vehicle, we first understand that all phenomena are empty, meditate on this fact, and finally realize it. This realization will bring to an end all confused appearances and the suffering of samsara they engender. In the Mahayana path, the ground is the emptiness of all phenomena, and an understanding of emptiness is developed through inferential valid cognition. Using logical arguments such as *one and many* and so on,[29] we determine that all things are merely collections of aggregates and therefore lack true existence. These logical arguments develop an intellectual understanding of emptiness, but they are very difficult to meditate on, and this makes the Mahayana a very long path. It is for this reason the sutras say that buddhahood can only be achieved through three innumerable eons of gathering the accumulations of merit and wisdom. It is the difficulty of refining this conceptual certainty of emptiness that makes for such a long path.

The third vehicle, the Vajrayāna, includes the profound path of mahāmudrā and reveals the ground in a different way. Especially in mahāmudrā meditation, the ground is not revealed through a logical analysis of external phenomena. In fact, whether trees, houses, and rocks are empty or not empty is not the main problem. The main problem and the cause of our suffering is our mind with its mistaken assumptions of solidity—its misapprehensions based on what seems to be real experience. As the sutras state, "Taming one's mind is the Buddha's teaching." All appearances arise in our mind, and so we make two basic assumptions: that our mind is solid and substantially existent and that external phenomena must be solid and existent as well because we experience them.

Since it is our own mind, we can look into it directly without looking at anything else. For example, we normally assume that our mind, like everything else, is seated somewhere in particular. We should then ask, Is our mind located in our head or in our heart, or somewhere between our head and feet? If we think our mind is located in a specific place, exactly where is it? When we look for a specific location of the mind, we cannot find it. Then we might think that even if the mind has no location, if it exists, surely it must have some kind of substantial characteristic. We should then ask, Does the mind have a shape? Is it round or triangular? and so on. When we look for its shape, we find nothing. When we look for its color, again we find nothing. In fact, when we look for any kind of substantial characteristics, we cannot find anything.

Now when we look at mind, we are not engaged in logical analysis. We are not drawing inferences about the mind and determining what it must logically be. Looking at mind is direct observation. We can directly observe our own mind simply because it is our own mind. And when we do so, we don't find anything. You might ask, Is it that we don't find anything because we didn't look hard enough or know how to look at the mind? Is it because the mind exists but it is so small that it can't be seen? Is it because the mind is perfectly transparent, like water, and we see through it and miss it? The answer is that we don't find the mind because the mind is empty. As the Buddha said, "All things are empty."

The three verses we looked at previously were primarily concerned with describing the manner in which we are confused. They illustrated how our confused perception sees things as existing while they actually don't exist. Second, in our confusion, we see something that actually exists as not existing. This first confusion is not recognizing the ground as actually being empty, and the second confusion is not recognizing that emptiness itself possesses inherent wisdom. While explaining how our confusion or ignorance arises, the verses also point out that the true nature of reality, the ground itself, is the unity of emptiness and lucidity.

A Brief Presentation of Path Mahāmudrā

A Song for the King turns here to a brief presentation of the path. The path is possible because ignorance by its very nature is false or incorrect. In other words, it is possible for the ocean to be calmed because the waves (ignorance) are not intrinsic to the ocean; the ocean is not necessarily made up of just waves. Since seeing two lamps comes from pressing on our eyes, when we stop doing it, we will no longer see two lamps and will see things as they are. In a similar way, we do not see the true nature of phenomena; nevertheless, the true nature is there and we simply fail to see it.

It is possible to eliminate confused appearances and discover the direct experience of the true nature. If the ground were inherently defective, there would be nothing we could do to change it. But since the ground itself does not consist of confused experiences, our ignorance can be removed and the true nature can be realized.

The methods employed in the tradition of the sutras and the tantras differ from each other. In the sutra path, one is mainly concerned with the true nature of all things, which is emptiness. Therefore, the focus of the sutra path is very vast, and we attempt to prove to ourselves that the nature of all phenomena without exception is emptiness. Whether we talk about the expanse and the emptiness of all things or the lucidity and wisdom of all things, they are indeed all-pervasive according to the sutras: emptiness is the nature of all phenomena without exception. It is quite possible to prove logically to ourselves that everything is emptiness, but it is comparatively difficult to meditate on these logical arguments using the sutra approach. In the practice of tantra, the focus is not as vast. Tantra is more concerned with profundity than with vastness, and therefore within the teachings, it is called the aspect of profundity. These instructions are not principally concerned with the empty nature of all phenomena, because it is not the emptiness of phenomena that poses the principal problem for us. Our problem stems from our mind.

Everything we experience—delight or depression, regret or guilt, sadness or happiness, enthusiasm, faith, or compassion—is rooted within our mind. We can analyze the nature of phenomena in the greatest detail, but it would still be very difficult to experience this emptiness directly. Within tantra, however, emptiness can be experienced directly through its principal practice of looking directly at our own mind. Whether we look at the mind itself or at the thoughts that arise as the mind's display, we can quickly and directly experience that mind is the manifestation of dharmatā (reality itself). Why is this so? While the nature of mind is the same as dharmatā, it is not evident in the experience of external objects; it is, however, evident in the experience of our own mind.

When the mind is scrutinized, we see that is has no shape, form, or color because it is empty. When we recognize this, we begin a process that will eventually culminate in the elimination of all our suffering. Even in the short term, this looking at the mind alleviates mental suffering. This is why we meditate on the mind.

We might ask, If we are concerned with the mind alone, why do we need to think about the view or the ground? We need the view because we must understand why we meditate. We do not meditate simply because it feels good or because we want to have great experiences. Nor do we meditate just because we want to feel peaceful and tranquil. We meditate because through meditation, it is possible to utterly eliminate from the mind all of our disturbing emotions. The purpose of meditation is to achieve complete elimination of the mind's afflictions. We meditate because our mind is innately capable of being utterly at peace, completely free of disturbing emotions, and also perfectly insightful and discerning.

We meditate to cleanse our mind. We do suffer from ignorance, but this confusion is temporary, since it is secondary to the mind's nature and not an intrinsic part of it. If we purify the mind through the practice of meditation, this ignorance can be removed. Further, since this ignorance is not fundamental to it, the mind does not disappear when the ignorance is removed. Our experience does not stop, nor is it superseded by a state of annihilation or nothingness. The qualities of the Buddha include the omniscient wisdom of the nature of phenomena and the wisdom of the variety of phenomena. The seed of this wisdom is innate to our mind, and we meditate in order to achieve it.

The path in general is a process that gradually transcends the confused appearances of samsara and culminates in their elimination. This is referred to as the fruition of the path. The path is usually presented as successive stages, like traveling from one place to another. Here, however, the song points out that the path does not truly consist of going from one state to another; it is more like returning to the original nature that we have failed to realize. By relinquishing bewilderment and confusion, we discover that nature. Since they are not intrinsic to the true nature of mind, the nature itself does not change: there is no real moving from one place, or one state, to another. We merely return to what was always there and see it without confusion or veils of ignorance.

The path has two aspects. The Third Karmapa, Rangjung Dorjé, wrote in his *Aspiration Prayer of Mahāmudrā:* "The meaning of the ground is the two truths beyond the extremes of permanence and annihilation." This means that we should recognize that the ground is beyond two extremes: the permanence of real existence and the annihilation of absolute nonexistence. The Third Karmapa continues: "The supreme path is the unity of the two accumulations, beyond the extremes of superimposition or denial." Superimposition and denial are ways of incorrectly understanding the nature of phenomena, that is, to have an incorrect perception of the ground. When we believe that something that does not actually exist does exist, that is the error of exaggeration. When we believe that something that actually does exist does not exist, that is the error of denial. The path, therefore, is the process of coming to see the ground as it is, free of these two extremes.

Seeing the ground as it actually is has two aspects called the two accumulations: the conceptual accumulation of merit and the nonconceptual accumulation of wisdom. The accumulation of wisdom is the process of developing a correct view that understands the ground and then continuing to meditate upon it. Of the two accumulations, this nonconceptual accumulation of wisdom is central and can only occur under the right conditions. The accumulation of merit, which involves concepts, is necessary to create the right conditions for the accumulation of wisdom, which transcends concepts. This gathering of merit can be done physically, verbally, or mentally, and it will facilitate and enhance our accumulation of wisdom. The path, therefore, consists of the integration of these two aspects.

This third verse discussed the nature of the path. The next verse in this brief presentation of the path uses three analogies to show why we can achieve realization by following the path.

The Wisdom Realizing Emptiness Purifies Ignorance

4.   Though diverse, rivers are one in the ocean.
     Though myriad, lies are overcome by a single truth.
     Though darkness is manifold,
     The rising of a single sun clears it away.

The first of the three analogies refers to rivers: "Though diverse, rivers are one in the ocean" means that all rivers eventually flow into the ocean. This analogy points to the fact that we undergo a wide variety of experiences produced by ignorance. Yet these myriad states of happiness and sadness, in their almost infinite variations, all have the same fundamental nature. Therefore, through the pursuit of one path, any confusion, no matter how vast or various, can be resolved.

The second analogy concerns lies and the truth: "Though myriad, lies are overcome by a single truth." This illustrates that no matter how many lies are told about something, once the truth is revealed, all those lies, even hundreds of them, are disproved and revealed as false. In one sense this example is an analogy, and in another sense it is a statement about the nature of confusion and realization. Whatever our ignorance and whatever our many varieties of confused appearances may be, if the true nature of phenomena is realized, then all our confusion can be removed, because ultimately it is false. In other words, realization of reality's truth is overcomes all possible misperceptions about the nature of reality.

From the perspective of the vast sutra path, this means that through meditation on dharmatā, confused and incorrect appearances can be effaced. From the perspective of the profound tantra, this means that through meditation on the nature of the mind, ignorance can be gradually eradicated. What is especially significant here is that the path has an effect: it actually brings us to fruition by eliminating ignorance.

The third analogy is of the sun and darkness: "Though darkness is manifold, the rising of a single sun clears it away." No matter how dark a place is, no matter how vast an area darkness covers, and no matter how long it has been dark, once the sun shines upon it, the darkness is eliminated in an instant. This illustrates the relationship between what is true (the sun) and what is false (the darkness). No matter how much confusion we experience, how long we have been experiencing it, or whether it manifests as a state of happiness or a state of misery, if we cultivate the path of meditation on the nature of phenomena, this ignorance in all of its variety, intensity, and duration can be removed and the true nature can be realized.

In this fourth verse, Saraha states that based on his realization and experience, there is no doubt that the path of mahāmudrā can remove ignorance. He asserts this to assure his disciples that it is possible, thereby encouraging them to pursue the path. To follow any path and move from one place to another, we need a map, which is based on people having actually traveled on that path. For example, if we want to go from one city to another, we have to make sure that we know how to get there so we will not take the wrong road and get lost. To prevent this, we usually obtain a set of directions or a map. Looking at it, we learn what local roads we need to take in order to get to the right highway. In mahāmudrā, we use a map that was produced by generation after generation of mahāsiddhas, all of whom began exactly like us, in a state of ordinary bewilderment. They pursued this path and achieved its result, the total elimination of ignorance and the full realization of mind's true nature. Their description of the path allows us not to get lost while traveling upon it.

Some may wonder if actual and accurate instructions for traversing the path still exist. The answer is that they do, and they have not been lost or diluted over time. In fact, each generation of mahāsiddhas has added further clarifications to the layout. This is the map that shows us how to find the path in the beginning, how to continue along the path once we have gained some degree of experience, and, finally, what kind of realization we can expect. We can find this spiritual map for the entire path in the books of instruction on the practice of mahāmudrā.

Developing Faith and Diligence

Faith and interest are the ground providing a basis for our entrance into Dharma. The protector Maitreya stated in the *Ornament of Clear Realization*[30] that faith is like the foundation. This means that if you want to grow anything, such as trees, grains, or flowers, you need the earth. In the same way, faith is like the ground from which all of the qualities of the path arise. From the very beginning, faith and interest in Dharma are very important.

Those who have entered the path of Dharma have naturally developed these qualities. First, they understood enough about the Dharma to have an interest in it. Then, through great exertion and austerity they pursued its practice and study. Nevertheless, they must continue to look carefully at the quality of their faith and interest. Interest can be stable or it can be temporary and ephemeral. Even a transitory interest in Dharma is good. However, it is produced by conditions and when those conditions change, interest can vanish. So we need to stabilize our interest and faith, and this is achieved by knowing the reasons for having faith in the Dharma in the first place.

A series of contemplations called the *four thoughts that turn the mind* are instrumental in developing interest and faith in the Dharma. By studying and reflecting on these, we come to understand the reasons for and the benefits of practicing Dharma and, by contrast, the defects of not practicing. Thinking about these four thoughts most carefully is especially important for beginners. In particular, the Buddha said that the contemplation of impermanence, which is the second of the four thoughts, is like the footprint of an elephant. An elephant's footprint was considered the best footprint, because not only is it very large, but it has a nice round, uniform shape, not elongated and strange like a human footprint. In the same way, the contemplation of impermanence is the best, as it brings about a more spacious and uniform state of mind. In the beginning, it is impermanence that inspires our faith and interest in Dharma. Afterward, it is impermanence that inspires and encourages diligence in practice. For example, people often come to me and say, "I'm really interested in Dharma, but I cannot make myself practice." Or, "I used to practice a lot, but now I just cannot make myself do it." Or, "I really want to practice, but somehow I cannot get it together. I cannot find the time or the circumstances." In all these cases, the remedy for this inability to generate the diligence to practice is contemplation of impermanence. When we find that our diligence is flagging, we should bring impermanence to mind and our practice will increase. When we find that we are losing faith, considering impermanence will help it return. So impermanence is important at the beginning and throughout the path as the means of overcoming the loss of faith and diligence.

By reflecting on these four thoughts that turn the mind, we initially develop a stable faith; continuing on the path, we are able to further stabilize, strengthen, and reinforce our faith as we practice. In this way, the faith we first generate and then develop is not a casual or uninformed faith. It is faith based upon the correct information about why we should practice the Dharma, so it is much stronger and more stable. This is the reason for continuing to contemplate the four thoughts throughout the length of our path.

The Two Paths

The actual path can be followed in two ways: through the path of method and through the path of liberation. In the Kagyü tradition, the path of liberation is mahāmudrā practice, and the path of method is the six yogas of Nāropa. To pursue the path of method, we begin by accumulating merit and wisdom and then purifying our obscurations. This is done through the preliminary practices, which consist of going for

The Four Thoughts That Turn the Mind

I. THE PRECIOUS HUMAN LIFE

First, contemplate the preciousness of a life free and
   well-favored.
Difficult to gain, it is easy to lose; now I must make it
   meaningful.

II. IMPERMANENCE

Second, the environment and the living beings therein are
   impermanent;
In particular, the life of beings is like a bubble.
The time of death is uncertain; when dead, this body will be
   a corpse.
At that time only Dharma will help, so I must practice with
   diligence.

III. KARMA AS CAUSE AND EFFECT

Third, when death comes, I will be helpless.
Because I create karma, I must abandon negative actions
And always devote myself to virtuous ones.
Thinking this, every day I will examine my mind stream.

IV. THE DEFECTS OF SAMSARA

Fourth, the places, friends, comforts, and wealth of samsara
Are the constant torment of the three sufferings,
Just like a feast before the executioner leads one into death.
Cutting desire and attachment, I must endeavor to attain
   enlightenment.

refuge and generating bodhicitta while doing prostrations, then medi-
tating on Vajrasattva, making mandala offerings, and practicing guru
yoga. After completing guru yoga and receiving the blessing of our
teacher and lineage, we engage in the practice of a meditational deity
(Tib. *yidam*). Through the generation and completion stages of this prac-
tice, we achieve realization. That is the path of means or method.

The path of liberation is the practice of mahāmudrā. It begins with the
stabilization of our wavering mind through the practice of tranquility
meditation. Then through insight meditation, which looks into the
nature of mind, mahāmudrā is accomplished. To facilitate and enhance
the practices of tranquility and insight, we must still engage in gathering
the two accumulations even while pursuing the path of liberation. The
accumulations serve to greatly enhance the practices of tranquility and
insight. When our practice of tranquility is unstable, it can be grounded
through these practices. When we lack insight, it can be generated by
these practices. Therefore, the path in either format conforms to what
was said by the Third Karmapa, Rangjung Dorjé, in his *Aspiration Prayer
of Mahāmudrā:* "The supreme path is that of the two accumulations,
beyond the extremes of exaggeration and denial." The principal path is
facilitated through gathering the accumulation of merit. Though the
path of means and the path of liberation may appear distinct, the nature
of the paths and what is to be realized by them is the same.

Mahāmudrā as a Modern Buddhist Practice

Since the paths of method and liberation have the same nature and lead
to the same result, it is possible to practice them in isolation or to com-
bine them. These days, especially in the West, the path of liberation will
be of the greatest benefit, because of the eighty-four mahāsiddhas, or
great masters, who arose during a time in the history of India when the
Dharma and the Vajrayāna flourished simultaneously. What they had in

common was that all of them practiced mahāmudrā and through it, all of them attained realization. Beyond that, their lifestyles varied tremendously. Some of them were in very high social positions like the powerful and wealthy King Indrabhuti. While fulfilling his responsibilities as a king and enjoying the luxury of his court life, he was able to practice mahāmudrā meditation and achieve complete awakening. We can infer from this example that mahāmudrā practice works in a situation of vast activity, tremendous responsibility, and great luxury.

Other mahāsiddhas were important scholars, of whom the best-known was Nāgārjuna, one of the greatest scholars in the history of Buddhism. Throughout his life, he composed an impressive number of treatises, which clarified for the first time various aspects of the Buddha's teachings. In his compositions Nāgārjuna refuted mistaken positions so skillfully that even those he refuted accepted his arguments. Due to his effectiveness, the Buddha's teachings spread far and wide. Nāgārjuna's impact was so far-reaching that he revolutionized Buddhist scholarship. Even non-Buddhist traditions in India were radically changed by his writing and his methods of reasoning. This tremendous influence was due to the precision of his reasoning, which was unprecedented. Though Nāgārjuna was busy teaching, composing, or debating, he still managed to achieve supreme siddhi in his lifetime through the practice of mahāmudrā. It is therefore evident that mahāmudrā can be practiced effectively in a busy life of scholarship. Other mahāsiddhas had common occupations, some of them quite lowly; for example, the great siddha Tilopa ground sesame seeds. Those with little time or wealth were also able to practice mahāmudrā and achieve full awakening.

If we look at our present situation, we can see that some practitioners are in high social positions with great responsibilities and living in great luxury; others have ordinary occupations, which keep them quite busy; and still others are academics, scholars, and so forth. The point of the example of the mahāsiddhas is that all of these types of people with their many different lifestyles can practice mahāmudrā effectively and can definitely achieve enlightenment. Furthermore, if the practice of mahāmudrā is combined with the practice of the preliminaries as a foundation, it will go very well.

A Brief Presentation of Fruition Mahāmudrā

AN EXAMPLE AND ITS MEANING

5. Though cloud banks take up water from the ocean
    And fill the earth again with descending rains,
    The ocean does not decrease; filling the whole sky, it remains full:
    There is no increase or decrease.

6. The Victorious Ones are filled with perfect qualities,
    Which all have the very same nature—spontaneous presence.
    From the natural display of the great sphere, living beings take
        birth and therein cease.
    In relation to this, there is no thing and no nonthing.[31]

The fifth and the sixth verses give a brief presentation of mahāmudrā's fruition. The fifth verse contains an analogy for the state of fruition and the sixth verse presents its meaning. Using the analogy of the ocean, Saraha illustrates that the fruition of mahāmudrā is a state beyond increase and decrease. Even though water from the ocean is taken up by clouds through evaporation and then sent down as rain, the ocean is never depleted of water; nor is the water of the ocean increased through rainfall, because the amount of water involved in the whole system remains constant. In the same way, through the pursuit of the path, we reach the goal of enlightenment and develop full realization of the nature of all phenomena or, one could say, we realize spontaneously present, coemergent wisdom. What we are realizing are the qualities of the ground, the unchanging basic nature, and so the qualities of the fruition, like the ocean, are unchanging. In other words, at fruition these qualities do not increase or decrease.

It is said in the *Uttaratantra*,[32] "There is nothing to be removed from this and there is nothing that needs to be added to this." When something perfect is perfectly seen, you will be perfectly liberated. There is no defect in the nature of your mind that needs to be removed. There are no qualities outside of it that need to be introduced into it. If you can look at this nature properly to see the nature as it is and you see this completely, then simply through this act, you will be completely liberated. This is the point of verse 6.

In summary, verses 1 to 3 explain the ground; verse 4 explains the path; and verses 5 and 6 explain the fruition of mahāmudrā.

Questions

Question: Rinpoche, you made some statements regarding generalized and linguistic abstractions and I was wondering if you could go over that again.

Rinpoche: I mentioned these as illustrations of how bewildered appearances occur within the mind. More specifically, I was talking about how we experience outside objects and perceive our thinking mind, without the mind and its object actually existing as two separate things. When an object experienced by one of the senses appears in our mind, what appears is a generalized image or likeness of that thing. For example, if we imagine our home right now, we will be able to create a fairly clear and detailed picture of the various rooms, our furniture, and so forth. In spite of the vividness of this experience and its great detail, none of these things are actually physically present within our mind. What is present is an image of it, a mere appearance. In the context of valid cognition, this is called a generalized or generic image abstracted from our experience.

I also mentioned that sometimes this image in our mind could be a generalized sound or a linguistic abstraction. For example, when the name of a person or the name of an object with which we are familiar comes to mind, that person or thing is not actually present, and yet the name of the person or thing brings up associations with it. Furthermore, when we think of the name, we have not actually heard the sound of the name. A linguistic abstraction is like an image of a sound. We did not actually hear that sound because someone did not actually say that name, and yet the image of that sound arose in our mind and brought with it all of the associations with the object or person we habitually refer to by using that word. These are all examples of how something can arise vividly in the mind—a clear image or a recollected sound, a name or a word—and yet it is empty of physical existence and is therefore an empty manifestation.

Question: Is this creation of generalized images true for the visualization of meditational deities?

Rinpoche: In the practice of the generation stage, the visualization of deities does involve the use of generalized images. However, the context of visualizing deities is different from our discussion here. The introduction of generalized images points to the fact that while we seem to see trees and rocks outside, what we imagine is not there. While we seem to hear in our mind the sound of a word or name, it is not there. By contrast, in the practice of the generation stage of the deity, we are mainly concerned with relative truth and not ultimate truth. We are mainly concerned with the aspect of lucidity and not the aspect of emptiness. In our discussion of the term *generalized image*, we are looking into emptiness.

Question: Rinpoche, it is my understanding that we are to come to mahāmudrā practice without concepts, without fabrication. Yet from hearing these wonderful Dharma teachings, I now have many concepts. I am expecting to have a certain experience in mahāmudrā that has been described as spacious, clear, and lucid. Now I feel that these concepts are a hindrance and a support. What to do with them? And if I do have an experience in doing mahāmudrā practice, how do I know if it is really a fabrication of my mind?

Rinpoche: The primary intent of mahāmudrā instruction is to teach us to be free of any attempt to control or alter the mind's nature. The instructions are that in meditation, we should be free of any wish to create or maintain any particular mental state. In the mahāmudrā tradition, the type of meditation in which we pursue the experience of trying to achieve a particular state of mind is known as rainbow meditation: we are pursuing something beautiful for the experience. The problem with this is that we are trying to bring about a certain positive experience. This involves conceptual contrivance and altering the mind—the very things that prevent us from experiencing mind's nature, which is not contrived and cannot be altered or changed. Therefore, instead of experiencing mind's nature, we experience whatever it is that we have created.

Mahāmudrā meditation is a direct experience of the mind as it is and not an attempt to alter or create it. The mind's nature does not have to be changed, and, actually, the true nature cannot be created or recreated. Nevertheless, this instruction does not mean that we should allow ourselves to be distracted by thoughts or disturbing emotions. The freedom from alteration does not mean allowing ourselves to be drawn away; it means freedom from the conceptually directed meditation of attempting to achieve a certain state. For example, while meditating we may think, "I must experience this emptiness. The mind is brilliant lucidity and I must perceive this lucidity." The primary intent of the instruction is to be free from this discursiveness.

With regard to your second question, it is difficult to ascertain immediately the nature of an experience in meditation. But over time, based on what happens to the experience, you will be able to tell whether it is an authentic experience of mind's nature or some kind of contrived experience. If the experience is of something contrived, it will gradually dissolve. That is why it is said, "Experience vanishes like the mist." So over time, if the experience does not develop but diminishes, that indicates that it was a temporary, or contrived, experience. However, if it gradually develops toward realization, this indicates that it was authentic. You will have very few questions about this true experience, because the wisdom of the experience itself will obviate theorizing questions about it.

Ground Mahāmudrā   3

T HE FIRST SIX VERSES of Saraha's song presented an overview of the
    ground, path, and fruition. Saraha now returns to the same sub-
jects, but in much greater detail. I apologize for the repetitious nature of
traditional Buddhist texts. The reason for this is that the initial presenta-
tion is a brief summary that serves as an introduction to the whole work.

Generally, in the context of the ground, path, and fruition, the under-
standing of the ground is presented in terms of the three aspects of prac-
tice: view, meditation, and conduct. The view is the general outlook of
the ground. The Third Karmapa, Rangjung Dorjé, wrote: "Confidence
in the view is the eradication of superimposition and denial with regard
to the ground." Previously, we saw that the ground is explained as the
way things really are and that not seeing this leads to ignorance. Through
the realization of mind's nature, a special certainty is generated within;
when we comprehend this, it becomes the view. The view is unmistaken
because it is not caught by the fault of superimposition, which is the
belief that something exists when it actually does not. Further, the view
is not mistaken because it is not caught by the fault of denial, the belief
that something that actually does exist does not.

The detailed presentation of the ground makes up fourteen stanzas.
The first four of these stanzas use incongruent analogies[33] to show that
craving or fixation must be given up. Generally, the type of craving that

is referred to in these verses is an attachment that can arise through the practice of meditation. This happens when we have an experience and then begin to desire its repetition and continuation. The reason such craving must be relinquished is that the purpose of meditation is to realize the nature of our mind. Attachment to any form of temporary or conditioned experience obstructs this realization, because what we are attempting to realize is not temporary or conditioned experiences but what transcends them.

Attachments to Be Abandoned in Meditation
ATTACHMENT TO CONDITIONED BLISS

7. Giving up genuine bliss, you take another path
    And place your hopes in conditioned bliss.
    Taking nectar in their mouth, bees come close,
    But not drinking, they are far from enjoyment.

There are four verses concerned with the problem of attachment to a temporary experience in meditation. The analogy used in the first of these stanzas is the analogy of bees taking nectar from flowers on the mountainsides and then not being able to consume it themselves. When bees take nectar from the flowers they find, they put it into their mouths, so they are very close to enjoying it. But they never actually do so. They give it to others, and therefore, from their point of view, their collection of the nectar is pointless. Unlike the bees, when practicing meditation, we must drink the ultimate nectar: we must realize the mind's nature. If we become attached to conditioned bliss, which is a temporary experience of intense well-being, then this attachment to a temporary state will prevent us from actually experiencing the true result of meditation practice. In this sense, our meditation becomes like bees collecting honey without consuming it.

This situation of being bound by attachment to experience can happen through the pursuit of meditation in general or, in particular, through practicing the techniques found on the path of method. Here, through working with the subtle channels and subtle winds of our body, we can generate experiences of bliss, extraordinary clarity, and nonthought. These experiences arise on the path of method, but they are not the goal of the path. The purpose of these experiences is merely to serve as methods leading to the recognition of mind's nature. The experiences themselves are not the point of meditation. Therefore, becoming attached to them prevents us from going toward our true goal.

In sum, whenever experiences of bliss, clarity, and nonconceptuality arise in meditation, it is important not to become attached to them. The situation is fundamentally the same whether the experiences arise through the path of method or through the practice of tranquility and insight. As long as we become attached to any meditation experience, we are like a bee that collects honey but never gets to consume it. The contrary is also true: if we are not attached to the experiences in meditation, we are like a bee that actually gets to consume the honey.

ATTACHMENT TO WHAT IS TO BE TAKEN OR GIVEN UP

8.   Having gone astray, the animals do not create suffering;
      On the basis of this human life, experts create suffering.
      On one hand, practitioners come to drink the nectar of space;
      On the other, experts remain very attached to objects.

The previous verse presented an analogy for relinquishing attachment to experiences in meditation. Verse 8 concerns discarding attachment to what is to be accepted and what is to be rejected. The analogy used here is of a clever person and a foolish person. However, in this case, the foolish person is the positive example and the clever person is the negative one.

The first two lines state: "Having gone astray, the animals do not create suffering; on the basis of this human life, experts create suffering." Normally we would think of animals as stupid and experts, human beings, as smart. But animals do not accumulate very much negative karma. Even predators such as lions and tigers kill to eat, and therefore, they do not really accumulate much negative karma because their motivation is not malicious. Furthermore, during their whole lives they do not kill as many beings as an expert can kill in one instant with a bomb. Often, human intelligence is used not for the good but as a cause of great tragedies and the accumulation of negative karma. Here, the analogy shows that under certain circumstances, it is better to be dumb than to be smart.

The second two lines of this verse explain what the analogy refers to. "On one hand, practitioners come to drink the nectar of space; on the other, experts remain very attached to objects." "Experts" here refers to those who are very learned in Dharma and therefore very skilled at rigorous logical analysis of phenomena. Such persons can be referred to as "Dharma professionals," and they correspond to the experts in the second line. The dumb animals in the first line are comparable to yogis or practitioners, who appear somewhat dumb or unsophisticated when compared to these clever individuals.

The experts use their intellect to analyze the nature of phenomena meticulously. The criticism here is not of the analysis itself; it is just that they never get to the point of applying what they discover in analysis to actual meditation practice. If the fruition that comes from logically analyzing phenomena is not used in meditation practice to develop an authentic experience of the mind's nature, then the heaps of knowledge and information accumulated are useless. On the other hand, a yogi rests his or her mind in meditation and thereby drinks the nectar of space. "Drinking the nectar of space" means coming to realize the nature of the mind, or dharmatā. Yogis, who are comparatively dumb, achieve the ultimate result. The point here is simply that meditation is more important than clever analysis. It is not saying that the logical analysis of phenomena is bad; on the contrary, it is good. But if it is never applied to practical experience, it is wasted.

It is for this reason that in Vajrayāna practice, the view is developed by means of direct valid cognition and not inferential valid cognition. These two types of valid cognition are two possible ways that the view can be generated, and therefore they are two possible foundations of the path. Using inferential valid cognition to ascertain the view involves strict logical analysis. Nāgārjuna carefully described this process in order to reveal emptiness as the true nature of all phenomena. In his system, one examines phenomena, including apparently solid objects, and proves through logical reasoning that they are empty.

Inferential valid cognition actually has two aspects: One is the analysis of the existence of self, and the other is the analysis of the existence of external phenomena. In the first case, what we are analyzing is that which we normally think of as "I" or "myself." We examine the characteristics of this imputed self and look to see if there is anything that possesses these characteristics. We also examine to see (1) if the self is located in or is identical to the body or (2) if the self is located in or is identical to the mind. With careful analysis, we discover that none of these are the case, because the self or "I" does not exist.

Through logical analysis, we can show that all phenomena can be broken down ever further into components.[34] Therefore, even the coarsest and most apparently solid phenomena are merely aggregates and thus have no true existence. This type of analysis generates a great conceptual certainty that emptiness is indeed the true nature of phenomena.

In their spiritual songs, Kagyü masters of the past have said that those who are learned in reasoning and scripture have lost the meaning of nonduality. What this means is that through the rigorous study of the scriptures and their commentaries and through the application of logical reasoning, we can develop a very refined conceptual understanding of the nature of phenomena. But having mastered this, we will not see the true nature itself, because it cannot be an object of conceptual understanding. The true nature cannot be realized through concepts.

For example, when logically examining mind's true nature, we determine that existence and nonexistence are mutually exclusive. Either something exists or it does not. But when we hold these two conditions as mutually exclusive, we are prevented from directly realizing that the true nature of phenomena is the unity of appearance and emptiness. The reason this unity cannot be apprehended intellectually was stated by Śāntideva in *A Guide to the Bodhisattva's Way of Life:* "Ultimate truth is not the object of the intellect because the intellect itself is relative truth." The intellect can only think, and ultimate truth cannot be grasped by thought. Only things that can be conceptualized are within the realm of relative truth. This means that all the clever thinking and analysis we do is not sufficient to lead us to the recognition of ultimate truth, even though ultimate truth is the object of the intellectual examination. Śāntideva continues: "Whereas we [practitioners] with the key of oral instructions put our finger right on it and take it as the path." It is the oral instructions[35] and not Madhyamaka analysis that allows us to identify the true nature as surely as if we could touch it with our fingertip.

The second way to develop the view, which is the one used most often in the Vajrayāna, is taking direct valid cognition as the path. In this approach, we do not analyze external phenomena or external objects; rather, we look directly at our mind. Furthermore, not only is the object of consideration different, but the manner of examining is different as well. When looking at, or for, the mind, we do not look for it with reasoning. We do not attempt to prove through logical analysis that the mind must be one thing or many things, and so on. We just look at it directly to observe its characteristics.

In order to understand how these approaches are actually implemented by Vajrayāna practitioners, we need to think of Dharma practice in three broad phases: hearing (or studying), contemplating (or thinking about), and meditating. When engaged in the first two stages of training—hearing and contemplating—we do not employ direct valid cognition but turn to inferential valid cognition, which is the rigorous application of logical analysis. This produces a decisive certainty about the nature of phenomena. Through this process, we become absolutely certain about what ultimate truth is like.

But when we begin to practice meditation, we do not employ inferential valid cognition; we use direct valid cognition. Inference is very effective in producing a decisive conceptual certainty, but it is very hard to apply this certainty to direct experience. It takes an extremely long time to refine it and develop actual wisdom. For this reason, the Buddha said, "It takes three periods of innumerable eons of gathering the accumulations to achieve buddhahood." Therefore, we do not use inference in the practice of meditation, but direct valid cognition.

In Vajrayāna, the view is established through what is called the view of direct experience, which refers to direct valid cognition. Through direct observation of the mind, we know how the mind is without having to infer or deduce it.

The Vajrayāna path leads to the state of great unity, the state of Vajradhara, in one lifetime and in one body. This leads to a question: If the Buddha said that it takes three periods of innumerable eons to achieve buddhahood, then the statement that one can achieve the same state in one lifetime and one body must be untrue. Or conversely, if it is true that one can achieve buddhahood in one lifetime and one body, then the Buddha's statement that it takes three periods of innumerable eons to achieve buddhahood must be untrue. In fact, both statements are true. It takes three periods of innumerable eons to achieve buddhahood if one takes a path based solely on inferential valid cognition. It takes so long and involves such gathering of the accumulations because there is great difficulty in implementing inferential valid cognition in practical experience. The statement that we can achieve buddhahood in just one lifetime with one body is found in the context of the uncommon oral instructions. These are all based on taking direct experience and direct valid cognition as the basis of the path. In the practice of mahāmudrā, the view is established through direct valid cognition; in the practices of the Vajrayāna, direct valid cognition is the tradition of the siddhas. I think this path is an excellent one for us to follow.

In this eighth verse a distinction is made between practitioners who come to drink the nectar of space and experts who remain attached to objects. The point being made here is very significant. The cultivation of the wisdom arising through hearing and contemplation is of great importance. But if we become attached to it and consider it as an end in itself, it becomes meaningless and useless, because the only function of this wisdom is to prepare us for the direct experience in meditation. By themselves, the wisdoms of hearing and contemplation cannot lead to buddhahood. We do need to cultivate these, but after having done so, we must actually engage in the practice of meditation. In sum, Saraha is saying not to waste the opportunity of this life in interminable analysis, but to practice meditation so that we can drink the nectar of space.

ATTACHMENT TO WHAT IS CONTAMINATED

9.   Bugs on excrement are attached to its smell
      And think the pure fragrance of sandalwood foul.
      Likewise, attached to dense ignorance, the source of samsara,
      Individuals toss away the transcendence of suffering.

The seventh stanza was an instruction to relinquish attachment to meditation experiences and to use meditation to recognize the mind's nature. The eighth verse was an instruction to relinquish attachment to the wisdom arising from hearing and contemplation and to go further into the actual practice of meditation.

The ninth verse contains the instruction to give up attachment to what is defiled. As long as we have this attachment, we will not aspire toward anything beyond it. The verse states: "Bugs on excrement are attached to its smell and think the pure fragrance of sandalwood foul." Dung beetles, who live in the midst of excrement, think that this smell is really good; if they were to smell something like sandalwood, which we would normally regard as pleasant, they would be disgusted by it. In the same way, those who are attached to dense ignorance, including the attachment to pleasures of this life, cast away the possibility of transcending suffering, and in this sense, they are like bugs.

Living in this world, we have no choice but to deal with the commonplace. The instruction here is not that we should try to avoid it but that we should not limit ourselves to the mundane. Do not be so concerned with the everyday world that you exclude Dharma from your experience, because if you were to do so, you would end up wasting your life.

ATTACHMENT TO SIGNS AND INDICATIONS

10.   The ignorant think an ox's hoofprint filled with water is the
        ocean and look for gems therein,
      Yet this water will soon evaporate. Likewise, those who take their
        passing experiences to be enlightenment
      Will not see the perfect qualities. By developing a stable and
        perfect mind,
      The mind clinging to passing experience as perfect will evaporate.

The tenth verse is an instruction to abandon attachment to extraordinary experiences and signs in our meditation practice. When we practice meditation, we are working with our mind in a different way, and so we start to experience thoughts and appearances we have not experienced before. We can become quite impressed with these experiences. We may have new thoughts or see things that we take as indications of attainment. If we become attached to these appearances, they become a diversion from the pursuit of a genuine path, because we have become attached to something that is conditioned and temporary. The first line reads: "The ignorant think an ox's hoofprint filled with water is the ocean and look for gems therein, yet this water will soon evaporate." Taking a transitory experience or vision that may occur during meditation to be real attainment is like mistaking a hoofprint filled with water for the ocean. Not only is the hoofprint much smaller than the ocean, it does not even possess any of the wonderful things found within the ocean, such as jewels. Further, a hoofprint full of water will evaporate, whereas the ocean will not. In the same way, these meditative experiences are transitory, and becoming attached to them will only turn us away from a true path.

The verse continues: "Likewise, those who take their passing experiences to be enlightenment will not see the perfect qualities. By developing a stable and perfect mind, the mind clinging to passing experience as perfect will evaporate." When we practice meditation, we can experience all sorts of things. We might see visions, we might hear extraordinary sounds, and we might experience cognitive states that are unprecedented. But none of these experiences have any use whatsoever in themselves. The only purpose of practice is to recognize the nature of mind. If, impressed with transitory experiences, we allow ourselves to be diverted from that single intention, we will be mistaking a hoofprint for the ocean.

Identifying the Meaning of the Ground

Within this extensive presentation of the ground, the previous four verses were all concerned with pointing out the danger of misunderstanding the ground and the need to abandon these errors. In this section we will look at verses 11 through 14, which by means of four analogies explain why the qualities of an authentic understanding of the ground can be developed and need to be developed.

REALIZATION WILL REMOVE FAULTS

11. Just as the ocean's salty water
     Taken into the clouds turns sweet,
     The stable mind works to benefit others;
     The poison of objects turns into healing nectar.

Verse 11 illustrates that if we realize the true nature of the mind, this realization itself will remove all defects and problems. These could be of various types—disturbing thoughts or emotions, experiences of intense sadness or regret. They can all be removed through the recognition of mind's nature in mahāmudrā practice. How this is possible is explained here through an analogy of ocean water. We cannot drink seawater because it is too salty. Nevertheless, after the ocean's water evaporates, gathers into clouds, and returns to the earth as rain, it has become pure. No longer salty, it is fit to drink.

The meaning of this analogy is as follows. We continually give rise to various forms of disturbing emotions. For example, when we encounter an external object that makes us angry, this experience of anger causes us to be unhappy. If we act on this anger, others can suffer as well. To give another example: When we are frustrated by the failure of our endeavors, we can become highly anxious and miserable, and this may last for our whole life. In each of these situations, it seems to us that the disturbing emotion or suffering that arises in our mind is very solid and powerful. Since it is so intense, it appears to be more powerful than we feel we are. However, if we actually look and meditate on the mind's nature, we discover that all the things arising in our mind—thoughts, disturbing emotions, sadness, and misery—are mere appearances. If we scrutinize them, looking to see what they really are and where they really are, we will discover they are empty of substance and location. When we look directly at the thoughts, disturbing emotions, and misery that arise in our mind, we cannot find where they are located or where they came from or whether they have a shape or color. We never find any of these qualities that all the objects seem to have.

Examining here means looking at the thought within the mind, not examining the object that inspired the thought or the condition that led to the disturbing emotion. It is scrutiny of the thought itself; we directly observe the emptiness of the thought. Whether we do this in the context of benefiting others—as the verse states, "the stable mind works to benefit others"—or simply in the context of benefiting ourselves, what happens when we see the nature of thoughts is that the previously poisonous quality of the thought, the disturbing emotion, or the suffering is transformed into a situation of great benefit. And so as the verse states, "the poison of objects turns into healing nectar." We believe that disturbing emotions are terrible, that thoughts are bad, and that sadness is a shame. But the nature of these conditions that arise in our mind is actually flawless bliss. Since we do not recognize their nature, we are afflicted by them. Actually, in and of themselves, thoughts and emotions are not bad, because their nature is peace. Nevertheless, as long as disturbing emotions arise as afflictions, they are, of course, a problem. When we recognize the nature of thoughts, disturbing emotions, or sadness, it is like experiencing a healing nectar. The poison of thoughts and disturbing emotions is transformed into amrita.

In the context of the gradual instruction of mahāmudrā, this process of scrutinizing thoughts is called looking at the mind within occurrence, or looking at the moving mind. It is normally preceded by the practice of looking at the mind within stillness. This latter practice means that when we are in a stable state of meditation, we look directly at our own mind. Specifically, we look to see where and what the mind is. Through this investigation we eventually discover that there is no location and no substance of mind to be found. In this way, we resolve experientially that the mind is empty.

This eleventh verse presents looking at the mind in motion. Occurrence, or movement, means that a thought occurs within the mind. The thought could be any kind of thought—an angry thought, a jealous thought, an arrogant thought, a desirous thought, a sad thought, a happy thought, or a compassionate thought. Whatever the content of the thought may be, when we recognize that a thought has arisen, we look directly at it. In looking at the thought, we see its nature and discover that it is like the nature of the mind itself: it has no location and no substance. It is empty. So through the practice of looking at the mind within the occurrence of thought, we transform the mind's apparent poison into healing nectar, which is its true nature.

Despite Fear, Realization Turns into Bliss

12. When you realize the ineffable, it is neither suffering nor bliss.
     When there is nothing to meditate upon, wisdom itself is bliss.
     Likewise, though thunder may evoke fear,
     The falling of rain makes harvests ripen.

This twelfth verse is concerned with the benefit of realizing the inexpressible or ineffable, which here refers to emptiness. When we use the word *emptiness* or *empty*, it can sound very threatening. Its literal meaning is "nothing," making it sound like annihilation, but the nature of emptiness is great peace or great bliss. We may incorrectly fear the realization of emptiness, believing that this realization will produce the annihilation of experience; however, the realization of emptiness is the realization of great peace and great tranquility. When the realization of emptiness occurs, it is different from what we fear it will be, because there is nothing within emptiness that inherently justifies the fear. Emptiness is not in and of itself negative or threatening.

The word *emptiness,* of course, connotes nothingness and makes us think of something like empty space, a mere absence, such as the absence of any qualities or content. But the emptiness of the mind is what is called "emptiness endowed with the best of all aspects." This means that while the mind is empty, it is not a voidness; rather, it is cognitive lucidity. This means, for example, that when you look at your mind, you do not find the mind, nor do you see thoughts in terms of their having a location or possessing substantial characteristics. The mind and the thoughts within the mind are empty but they are not nothing, because there is an unceasing display of mind's cognition. This shows that the absence of substantial existence does not mean that the mind is dead like a stone. For this reason, the realization of this absence of true existence does not cause the cessation of experience.

While being empty of any kind of substantial existence, the mind remains an unceasing awareness. Yet, when you look for it, you cannot find it anywhere; you cannot find anything substantial because the mind is empty. It is also unchanging. If the mind were not empty, if the mind had solidity or substantial existence, it would definitely change. Often called "the inexpressible" or "that which is beyond intellect," the mind's emptiness is the reason that the mind is unchanging. And because the mind is unchanging, its nature is great bliss.

The analogy in verse 12 is the sound of thunder, which represents emptiness, or more precisely, our concept of emptiness. A child, for example, may be frightened by the sound of thunder and may perceive it as threat-ening. But when you think about it, thunder is a good thing, because thunder is a sign of rain, which ripens the crops. In the same way, while we might think of emptiness as threatening and negative, in fact its nature is great bliss, and therefore the realization of emptiness is very positive.

Appearance and Emptiness Are Nondual

13. First a thing and in the end a nonthing—neither is established;
        likewise, there is nothing other than these two.[36]
     There is no place to abide in the beginning, middle, or end.
     For those whose minds are obscured by continual concepts,
     Emptiness and compassion are expressed in words.

The next verse is concerned with the lack of an inherent substance in the arising, abiding, and cessation of thoughts. Or we could say that it deals with the unity of appearance and emptiness, which then brings forth the realization of the unity of emptiness and compassion.

When we consider the nature of mind or the essential nature of the thoughts that arise in the mind, we assume that these things must have begun somehow and somewhere. They must dwell somewhere and at some point they must cease. But when we actually look at how a thought arises and what actually happens, we don't find anything creating the thought, nor do we find the location of this arising. When we look for the characteristics that a thought might possess, such as color and shape, we do not find them. When we look to see where the thought is, even though it is vividly present within the mind, we cannot find it anywhere. The thought is not specifically located in any place within the body nor outside the body nor in some area in between. We must conclude that not only does the thought not truly arise, but it also does not abide or rest anywhere.

Finally, when a thought disappears, we look to see what really happens. Where does it go? We do not find anything. In this way, we are brought to the conclusion that thoughts do not truly arise, do not truly abide, and do not truly cease. Whether recognized or not, the nature of our mind has always been just this. It is not that the discovery of this nature makes the mind empty, because the mind has always been so. The problem is that we have never looked into our mind. We have always turned and looked outward, or away from it. This is the meaning of the thirteenth verse.

Verse 13 also answers this question: What qualities are produced by meditation on emptiness? The purpose of Dharma is to help others, and the root of this is compassion. But if all things are empty and if the emptiness of things is realized, is there then no object and therefore no root of compassion? This verse answers that question in the negative. As the Third Karmapa, Rangjung Dorjé, pointed out in his *Aspiration Prayer of Mahāmudrā:* "The very recognition of emptiness itself is the root of compassion." This is because the realization of mind's empty nature and the realization of phenomena's empty nature produces a state of well-being and tranquility in the mind. Disturbing emotions and suffering are pacified, and this causes all manner of positive qualities to develop within the mind. When we realize the true nature of mind, we gain the understanding that all beings without exception possess this same nature, this same potential to achieve all of the positive qualities through realization. At the same time, we realize that only those few fortunate individuals who recognize the nature of mind have all their suffering pacified and so compassion arises for those who have not attained this realization.

In general, we do not look at our mind and, therefore, do not recognize the nature of the mind and the nature of the thoughts. Rather, we are caught up by these thoughts, which then generate disturbing emotions, which lead to suffering. Since the basic nature of ordinary beings is the same as the nature of those who have realized mind's nature, we come to see that all of this suffering is really unnecessary: since beings possess this nature, they do not need to suffer at all. This recognition is why the realization of emptiness is the root of compassion. The Third Karmapa wrote: "May intolerable compassion be born in my mind through the realization of emptiness." The compassion that is born through realization is not merely words but intolerably intense.

HOW AN EXPERT DIFFERS FROM A DUNCE

14. Just as the nectar dwelling within a flower
     Is known by the bumblebee,
     The fortunate toss away neither existence nor nirvana.
     Like them, the ignorant should fully understand.

This verse is concerned with the fact that even though all beings without exception possess the same nature of mind, the mere possession of this buddha nature is not enough. It must be thought about and meditated upon. Saraha illustrates this with the analogy of the fortunate and the ignorant, or a wise person and a foolish person. In contrast to verse 8, the expert (here the fortunate one) represents the positive side and the foolish person the negative one. The analogy is the following. In a lake there is a lotus flower and in the midst of that lotus flower there is nectar, the potential for honey. A bee, representing the wise person, recognizes the presence of the nectar within the lotus flower and drinks its nectar.

In that same way, knowing about the presence of mind's nature, a learned person meditates on it and realizes it. On the other hand, the foolish person is like a frog. A frog lives in the lake adjacent to the lotus flower but doesn't know about the nectar within the flower and therefore does not enjoy its delicious taste. The frog illustrates that while all beings have the same nature of mind, when they do not know about it, they do not meditate on it and therefore do not realize it.

The last four verses have explained why the proper practice of the path will lead to realization. In the next set of four verses, we are going to look at what should be abandoned and what should be realized through combining congruent and incongruent analogies.

Indicating the Essential Nature

Nonattachment to What Is Untrue

15.   Just as an image appears on the mirror's surface,
      Where the ignorant look in their lack of knowledge,
      So the mind that throws away the truth
      Relies on many concepts that are not true.

This verse uses the analogy of a mirror's reflection to instruct us about abandoning our belief in and fixation on the reality of impure appearances. According to the analogy, if a small child who does not know about mirrors looks at his or her reflection, he or she may think that there is actually another child there. The child becomes attached to the reflection, thinking that it is a potential friend or playmate, and yet it is a mere reflection and nothing to be attached to. Similarly, when a monkey looks in a mirror, it sees its reflection as another monkey, who is a potential threat or competitor, and so the monkey bares its teeth and ferociously glares at its own reflection.

Just as the reflection in a mirror is not the actual presence of an object evoking attachment or aggression, in the same way, what appears in the mind is also not an object of attachment or aversion. Whether we are speaking of reflections or what appears within the mind, none of them have any intrinsic reality. Failing to understand this, we take them to be real. For example, when anger arises in our mind and we look at its nature, we can see that this anger has no true existence. However, if we do not look at the nature of the anger, it will seem real and thereby overwhelm us. When unhappiness arises in our mind, if we look at its nature, we see that it has no substantial characteristics—no color, shape, form, and so on. But if we never look at its nature, we will not recognize its lack of reality and will thereby come under its control.

It is important not to be caught by disturbing emotions appearing in our mind, because if we follow them, they will engulf us. If we are caught up by unhappiness or regret, it will oppress us with sadness. To keep from being overpowered by the afflictions, we should just look at the nature of whatever is arising in our mind.

If we think the reflections in the mirror are real, they will enslave us. If we follow after the disturbing emotions and mental states that arise within us, we become their servant, losing our freedom and control. However, if we recognize their nature, we will realize that it is peace and bliss. Therefore, to achieve realization, it is necessary to understand that these disturbing emotions and mental states do not ultimately exist; they are mere appearances like the images in a mirror. In mahāmudrā practice, we come to know the true nature of these mental states not by inference but through direct observation.

CONTINUOUS MEDITATIVE CONCENTRATION

16. Though the fragrance of a flower has no form,
    It clearly pervades everywhere.
    Likewise, through the formless nature
    The circles of the mandalas will be known.[37]

The previous verse instructed us not to be attached to appearances, disturbing emotions, and mental states. The sixteenth verse points out that we must recognize dharmatā, which can be recognized even though it is not a substantial entity. From the very beginning, dharmatā, the nature of mind, has been emptiness, and, consequently, it has no substantial existence. Nevertheless, we can familiarize ourselves with dharmatā and realize it, thereby achieving the final fruition. While it can be experienced and realized, dharmatā cannot be perceived by the senses, because it has no substantial characteristics.

The analogy presented in this verse is the fragrance of flowers. If flowers are present in one room, their fragrance will waft into the adjacent rooms. If you are in a neighboring room, however, you will not see flowers even though the room you are in is filled with their fragrance. In the same way, having no form and being empty, dharmatā cannot be perceived in the usual way. Yet in mahāmudrā practice, you can experience this emptiness through your direct observation of the mind, which is not, however, observation in the usual sense. Furthermore, in the practice of mahāmudrā, we are not attempting to transform something that exists into something that does not exist, nor to transform something that does not exist into something that does exist. This nature is the inherent emptiness of all phenomena and of the mind in particular. This emptiness, which we observe in the mind, is not a dead emptiness or a voidness, because it also has luminous clarity or wisdom. While it is emptiness, it is also lucidity, and while it is lucidity, it is also empty. This is the nature of mind that must be known. Although it has no substantial form or existence, it can be experienced because of its luminous clarity. It is this that must be understood, and it is this nature that must be realized. When the mind's nature is recognized, the result is the manifestation of the three bodies, or the arising of the mandala of the three kāyas—the dharmakāya, sambhogakāya, and nirmāṇakāya.

Through the recognition that mind itself is unborn and empty, what must be abandoned is abandoned. This can happen because we recognize that what is to be abandoned has no true existence. Through this recognition, it is liberated by its own nature. Further, when the nature of mind is recognized, we realize not just its emptiness but also its lucidity. By recognizing the lucidity, we attain what must be attained, which is the dharmakāya.

The qualities of the dharmakāya are wisdom, loving-kindness, and the ability to protect. In its wisdom, the dharmakāya knows the ultimate truth. Having realized that ultimate nature, it sees the nature of all things just as it is, which is called the wisdom of the true nature of phenomena. Does the dharmakāya know only the absolute nature of things? No, it also knows the manifestations, the variety of the appearances of all phenomena. It knows the characteristics of all appearances and it knows that these appearances are confusion. So this wisdom sees dharmatā, or emptiness, and it also knows the ignorance of beings. This wisdom that knows the bewilderment of beings is called the wisdom of the variety of phenomena, or we could say the wisdom that knows the variety of all the appearances of relative truth.

An analogy for this is the following. Imagine that a person is lying asleep in bed and dreaming. Beside the sleeping person is a second person with clairvoyance, who is awake and fully aware of the content of the other person's dreams. The person with extrasensory perception knows that the person who is asleep is just asleep in bed and what that person is experiencing is just dreams. In the same way, a buddha personally does not experience ignorance or confusion but does see the ignorance of beings in all its detail and variety.

The dharmakāya possesses this excellent wisdom, which knows both ultimate truth and relative truth. Through this excellent and consummate wisdom, the Buddha naturally possesses great compassion for all beings who are suffering, for those who are carried away by their disturbing emotions, and even for those who are not presently suffering but are still confused. So the dharmakāya, the mind of a buddha, possesses not only this twofold wisdom but also consummate loving-kindness. Possessing this wisdom and loving-kindness, a buddha sees all beings with compassion. The dharmakāya can protect beings: the Buddha is able to help and benefit them through an immense variety of methods. In sum, the mind of the Buddha, the dharmakāya, possesses the qualities of wisdom, loving-kindness, and ability to help, which are the result of the path.

From the dharmakāya arise the sambhogakāya and nirmāṇakāya, which together make up the rūpakayā, or form body. The dharmakāya with its qualities of wisdom, loving-kindness, and ability to protect is considered the causal condition for these other two form bodies. The dharmakāya, however, cannot be visited or experienced by ordinary sentient beings, and so it emanates the form bodies. For those with purified karma, bodhisattvas abiding on any of the ten bodhisattva levels, the dharmakāya manifests as the sambhogakāya. The sambhogakāya, or perfect enjoyment body, is called the enjoyment body because in the sambhogakāya realm, Dharma is continually taught and one never needs to pass into parinirvana. In that way, the sambhogakāya is endowed with what are called the five certainties of the perfect teacher, teachings, retinue, place, and time.

For those individuals with impure karma, like most of us ordinary beings who cannot visit or encounter the sambhogakāya, the dharma-kāya emanates as the nirmāṇakāya, which is relatively impure. An example of the nirmāṇakāya is a buddha who comes into the world, performs the twelve deeds of a buddha, and teaches ordinary beings, as the historical Śākyamuni Buddha did. In sum, the three kāyas arise as a result of having meditated on the true nature.

HOW HABITS REIFY CONCEPTS

17. When a wintry wind strikes and stirs up water,
     Though soft, it takes the form of stone.

When concepts attempt to disturb mind's nature, where igno-
    rance cannot take form,
Appearances become very dense and solid.

The seventeenth verse illustrates that all appearances are the appearances
of the mind. Earth, stones, mountains, rocks, and so forth, all seem very
solid to us, so it is quite hard to understand how these things could be
merely the appearances of our mind. *The Ocean of Definitive Meaning*
points this out in stages: First it shows that appearances are mind; then
that mind is emptiness; further, that emptiness is spontaneously present;
and finally, that spontaneous presence is liberated in and of itself. The
subject of this verse is this same point. While earth, mountains, and
rocks in their true nature are no different from our mind, in terms of
how they appear, they seem vast, huge, and very solid. We might won-
der, How can our mind encompass and perceive what is so big and so
apparently solid? The analogy here is of water and ice. When it is not
frozen, water is a liquid; but when a body of water is subjected to a very
cold wind, it freezes and becomes ice, which is hard like stone. Nor-
mally we don't think of water as being hard, and yet ice is water and it
is hard.

In this same way, when our mind is disturbed by ignorance and dis-
turbing emotions, which resemble the cold wind, it produces coarse
thoughts. The gradual production of coarser and coarser thoughts,
which entail coarser and coarser modes of appearance, corresponds to the
gradual freezing of the water. These coarse thoughts cause the solid
appearance of earth and mountains, even though the thoughts them-
selves began as mere insubstantial things.

In sum, the seventeenth verse is a generalized presentation of the fact
that appearances are mind.

MIND IS NOT AFFECTED BY STAINS

18.   The true nature of any state of mind is free of flaws
      And unaffected by the mire of existence and nirvana.
      Even so, if a supreme gem is placed in a swamp,
      Its radiance will not be clear.

The analogy presented here is of a jewel that has somehow fallen into a swamp. The jewel itself has excellent color and shape and is completely pure in being a jewel. It does not degenerate at all while mired in the swamp; it remains exactly what it was. On the other hand, it can't be used. The jewel's qualities are not apparent because it is concealed. If the jewel is removed from the swamp and the mud is cleaned away, the jewel will be a perfect jewel and can be used appropriately. In the same way, as long as our mind is immersed in bewildered appearances, we cannot gain access to and make use of the mind's innate qualities. Through meditation, however, if we can separate the mind from ignorance, we will be able to make use of the innate qualities of the mind to engage in effortless and spontaneous benefit for ourselves and others.

Although the mind is empty, it is not empty in the sense of being a voidness. The mind's basic nature is simultaneously emptiness and cognitive lucidity. This nature has never been damaged or even affected by all the appearances, confusion, and ignorance within the three realms of samsara. So we have to ask, Is liberation from samsara actually effecting a change in the mind at all? It is not. From the very beginning the mind has been empty and lucid.

In meditation, therefore, we are not trying to change what the mind is; we are not trying to make what is not empty into something that is empty or to make something that is not lucid into something that is lucid. All we are doing in the practice of meditation is experiencing the mind as it is and as it always has been. When the mind is experienced and finally realized, that is liberation. There is no need to change the mind's nature, because the nature of the mind has never been affected by any confusion.

Often the nature of the mind is called buddha nature or sugatagarbha ("the essential nature of those gone to bliss"). When the term *sugata-garbha* is used, even though it refers to the nature of our own mind, it is thought of as a high state, as something very distant from us and unapproachable. It is therefore important to understand what sugata-garbha really means. *Sugata* means "those gone to bliss." The syllable *su* here is "bliss," which means that if you recognize and realize the nature of mind, you eliminate the suffering of samsara: the result of realizing the mind's nature is bliss. *Gata,* or "gone," means that innumerable buddhas have appeared and all of them have achieved enlightenment through realizing the nature of their mind and thereby attaining the bliss of full awakening.

All of the buddhas began as confused, bewildered sentient beings. They transcended the ignorance and suffering of samsara and entered into bliss. It is up to us now to follow the example of the buddhas and realize the nature of our mind and discover this indwelling bliss. Do we have the ability to do so? Yes, we have the innate capacity to follow and emulate those who have gone to bliss. If we lacked some qualities or abilities that they had, we might not be able to do it, but in the nature of our mind, we have everything that they ever had or have. Since we have what they have and they accomplished full awakening, we can do it also. This is why the nature of the mind is called the essential nature of those gone to bliss.

The *Uttaratantra* states: "Like a jewel, like space, and like pure water, it is continually free of disturbance." When a jewel is purified and the dirt that surrounds it is removed, the nature of the jewel itself does not change. The jewel was always a jewel in its nature or composition. Like-wise, when clouds disappear from the sky, the space of the sky does not undergo any change. The space was not inherently affected or polluted in its nature by the presence of the clouds. The third example is water. Water in itself is just pure water; it only becomes polluted when sediment is mixed with it. But even so, the water itself remains just water. Muddy water is water combined with something else, but the water is not in itself changed or damaged by the presence of the sediment.

In the same way, while our mind is afflicted and obscured by ignorance, disturbing emotions, and thoughts, the nature of the mind is not touched by their presence. However, when these obscurations are present, the qualities of the mind's nature will not be evident. So it says in the verse, "Even so, if a supreme gem is placed in a swamp, its radiance will not be clear."

The Dependent Arising of Cause and Effect
THE BASIS FOR SAMSARA AND NIRVANA

19.   When stupidity is clear, wisdom is unclear.
      When stupidity is clear, suffering is clear.
      Like this, from a seed, a seedling arises;
      With this seedling as a cause, offshoots appear.

This verse describes why we wander in samsara and how the confused appearances of samsara increase and spread. All samsara begins with ignorance, and in this verse, ignorance is referred to as a state of stupidity. By its nature, stupidity is unclear. It is an absence of knowledge, a lack of recognizing ultimate truth, which could be called a mere lack of clarity. However, simultaneous with that lack of recognition, there is a great clarity of ignorance in the projection of relative truth.[38] As samsara increases, it becomes clearer and clearer.

The basic nature that lies within every living being can be called the sugatagarbha or the dharmadhātu. Dharmadhātu refers primarily to the aspect of emptiness, and sugatagarbha refers primarily to the aspect of wisdom. The inability to recognize this basic nature of mind is called ignorance. It is the beginning of the eighth (ālaya) consciousness.[39] This failure to recognize the mind's nature occurs because the empty aspect of the mind's nature is not recognized due to the appearance of its lucid aspect. This causes ignorance and the arising of the eighth consciousness along with the habits it holds, which produce confused appearances. As these bewildered appearances increase, from the eighth consciousness arise the afflicted seventh consciousness and then the six functioning consciousnesses (the five sensory consciousnesses and the mental consciousness). At that point, the structure of the bewildered appearances of samsara is fully established. This process of intensification is described in the verse: "When stupidity is clear, wisdom is unclear." As the stupidity of samsara becomes more and more vivid and distinct, the underlying wisdom becomes less and less clear and more and more obscured. This is the same idea expressed in the previous verse with the lines "If a supreme gem is placed in a swamp, its radiance will not be clear." The radiance of the wisdom is obscured by the intensity of the stupidity.

When the mind is bewildered, the ālaya consciousness begins to accumulate negative habits and tendencies. The ālaya consciousness itself is not confused; it is mere cognitive lucidity. Nevertheless, it functions as the foundation for accumulating negative habits and for misperceiving the existence of the self. When we have this incorrect view that takes the self to exist, we also develop the incorrect view that the other exists as well. Through the increase of negative habits, based on thinking that a self and other exist, negative karmic latencies enter the ālaya consciousness, and this leads to the arising of the other seven consciousnesses.

Even though they are nonconceptual consciousnesses, the five sense consciousnesses arise as the result of habits accrued in the ālaya consciousness. The five sense consciousnesses are limited to perceiving a specific sensory input; for example, the eye consciousness just sees, the ear consciousness just hears, and so forth. The sensory consciousnesses do not appraise, recognize, judge, or in any way conceptualize what they see, hear, and so on. The sixth consciousness, the mental consciousness, is the consciousness that appraises, identifies, and judges what is perceived by the five sense consciousnesses. Therefore, it is the sixth consciousness that makes errors, such as believing different things to be essentially one and the same.

With the development of all eight consciousnesses, there is a state of full-blown ignorance, which is clear. The verse reads: "When stupidity is clear, wisdom is unclear." When wisdom is clear, the nature of the mind is realized. But when bewilderment, stupidity, and ignorance are clear, the true nature of mind is obscured. This leads to disturbing emotions, which in turn lead to the accumulation of negative karma, which then leads to suffering. Strictly speaking, not everything that results from actions causes suffering, because actions are of different types (positive, negative, and neutral) and so their results may be different. Nonetheless, directly or indirectly, the result of the disturbing emotions is suffering. For example, being very ill is obviously suffering and is called the suffering of suffering. But even an experience of happiness or well-being will change into a state of suffering because it is impermanent. In this sense, even states of temporary well-being are called the suffering of change. Furthermore, the pervasive environment of impermanence in which we live causes everything to turn eventually into suffering; this is called all-pervasive suffering. These three types of suffering are the result of the bewildered projections or appearances of samsara.

This verse presents an analogy to illustrate how the progressive intensification of stupidity causes suffering: "From a seed, a seedling arises; with this seedling as a cause, offshoots appear." Ignorance is the seed. When it is planted in the ground, it produces a seedling, from which emerges a stalk, and eventually branches grow from the stalk. In the same way, through increasing stupidity, we begin to suffer. This suffering keeps us in the midst of samsaric appearances, which always entail suffering in one way or another. Sometimes we experience the suffering of suffering, sometimes we experience the suffering of change, and sometimes we experience all-pervasive suffering. But we always experience suffering.

The verse also shows us, by implication, how to put an end to suffering. Everyone wants to stop suffering. Since the immediate cause of suffering is the disturbing emotions, it is clear that in order to get rid of the three kinds of suffering, we have to eliminate the disturbing emotions. When we look for the cause of disturbing emotions, we see that it is ignorance; obviously, we have to get rid of our ignorance if we want to lose these disturbing emotions. Remember that ignorance began with not seeing dharmatā, the true nature of our mind. So the remedy for ignorance is evident: seeing our mind's true nature.

If we see the true nature of dharmatā, then ignorance and bewilderment will vanish. Within the sutras, which emphasize vastness, we would refer to this nature as the dharmatā, the nature of all things, often explained as the unity of space and wisdom. Within the secret mantra, or the Vajrayāna, which emphasizes profundity and not so much the vast scope of the mind's nature, we would refer to this as the nature of our mind. We can also think of our mind as the nature of the sixth consciousness or the nature of the eighth consciousness. In either case, it is through looking at the nature of our mind that ignorance will be removed. We are bewildered and ignorant, because we have never looked into and realized this true nature. If we directly recognize it, we will eliminate ignorance, which is like the seed, and so the seedling will not grow, the stalk will not appear, and the branches will not develop.

TRANSCENDING ANALYSIS

20.   In analyzing the mind with the reasoning of being neither one nor
      many,
      If you discard the clear aspect of mind's nature, you will descend
      to the lower realms;
      While gazing at that suffering, you fall into its bottomless pit.
      How could one have anything but compassion for this?

This verse is concerned with the relationship between the wisdom aris-
ing from hearing and contemplation and then from meditation. It is
concerned with showing that the wisdom of meditation is more impor-
tant than the wisdom of hearing and the wisdom of contemplation. By
cultivating these two, we can establish that emptiness is the nature of
phenomena. To do this we employ various modes of logical analysis to
show that coarse external objects are merely collections or aggregates of
the subtle objects and that subtle objects themselves are aggregates and
so on until we show that things have no true existence.

   This argument based on the aggregates can also be applied to the mind
to show that it does not exist as the entity it appears to be. In the con-
text of hearing and thinking, there are the four or five great logical argu-
ments within the Middle Way school. These arguments are the refutation
of things being truly one or many, the refutation of production through
the four extremes, and so forth. Going through these logical arguments
definitely helps us to understand emptiness. But this process only pro-
duces an intellectual certainty. If you retain attachment to that concep-
tual certainty of emptiness, you will prevent that conceptual view from
performing its true function: to generate certainty that emptiness is the
nature of all things so that you are inspired to meditate on it and expe-
rience it directly. If you do not practice meditation, you will not be able
to relinquish attachment to that mere conceptual certainty, which can be
relinquished only through this third wisdom arising from meditation.

Compared to the other two, which are based on inferential cognition, this wisdom is very clear because it is based on direct valid cognition. Therefore the stanza says, "In analyzing the mind with the reasoning of being neither one nor many, if you discard the clear aspect of mind's nature…." "Clear" here refers to the clarity of the wisdom that arises from meditation. So if you remain attached to the conceptual view gained through logical analysis, you will not be able to transcend the bewildered appearances of samsara and will continue to live in cyclic existence.

The next lines state: "While gazing at that suffering, you fall into its bottomless pit. How could one have anything but compassion for this?" These lines point to the situation we have just discussed: After engendering certainty, you remain bound to it and do not practice meditation. This is like someone who knowingly jumps into a bottomless pit, a classic metaphor for samsara. Beings are constantly jumping into that pit, but they do so without knowing what they are doing. What is even more tragic, however, is when someone who knows it is a bottomless pit still jumps in. This is what you are doing if you stay attached to the conceptual certainty achieved through analysis and thereby do not practice meditation.

The text implies that we should not work with the Middle Way logical arguments but just practice meditation; however, it is helpful from time to time to study these logical arguments without becoming attached to them. The problem is not the logical methods or the certainty they produce but our attachment to them. For example, Milarepa said to Gampopa: "While meditating on mahāmudrā, do not engage in logical analysis. Nonconceptual wisdom will vanish if you do." It is the neglect of direct experience in the practice of meditation that is the problem. In sum, this verse counsels us not to become so attached to the logical analysis of external phenomena that we ignore the practice of meditation and the development of direct experience.

Questions

Question: Rinpoche, I have a question about the three types of wisdom related to hearing, contemplating, and meditating. What kind of meditation is this? If you meditate on emptiness, is it a form of tranquility meditation? What kind of meditation is it if you have analyzed a thing? What to do when you meditate like that?

Rinpoche: Inferential valid cognition establishes the view through analyzing the lack of existence of the object. This meditation is helpful because by gradually becoming certain that an object is not real, you will be less likely to be fixated on it. But inferential valid cognition is not sufficient to bring about liberation.

In order to achieve liberation, we need to apply the techniques of meditation, which are based on direct valid cognition. When a thought arises repeatedly—whether it is a thought of attachment or dislike or anything else—if you apply the approach of direct valid cognition, you do not consider what the thought is about, nor do you attempt to analyze the object of thought to determine its reality or unreality. In direct valid cognition, you look at the thought itself. We generally tend to think that thoughts arise and, after they have arisen, they are truly present. In this method of looking directly at the thought, we look to see how and where it arises, how and where it abides, then where it dissolves.

Question: Rinpoche, would you speak about the original source of this ignorance? How and why does it arise?

Rinpoche: Ignorance can be understood in different ways. The literal meaning of the word (Tib. *ma rig pa*) is "absence of knowledge." It can also mean "absence of luminous clarity." What it refers to is not recognizing mind's nature. We think of the mind as obscured, as it lacks a lucid recognition of its own nature. Nevertheless, the defining characteristic of mind is luminous clarity. So we have to say that from one perspective, our mind is dull and obscured and from another, it is intensely lucid. Usually the mind is lucid with regard to relative truth and ignorant of ultimate truth. This is true because mind has two characteristics. The nature of mind is emptiness, but unlike space, the emptiness of mind is not a void or nothingness. The other defining characteristic of mind is cognitive lucidity, inseparable from the mind's emptiness. It is the cognitive lucidity of mind that is the source of the whole variety of appearance, or experience, for that mind. Ignorance arises due to the intensity of the cognitive lucidity. It is so strong that it somehow conceals or outshines the emptiness, and so the mind fails to recognize its own empty nature. That failure, in turn, causes us to misapprehend our experience.

It's a little bit like watching television. When we look at a television, what we are seeing are dots and colors on the screen. The vividness and clarity of these colors allows us to perceive what they are supposed to represent. When we watch a television program, we have no trouble identifying places, persons, animals, mountains, and so on. Through becoming involved with the program, we identify with what we are seeing and begin to feel an emotional response. Actually, what we are looking at are not places, persons, animals, or mountains, but points of light on a tube in a little box. The confusion that is necessary to enjoy a television program is similar to bewilderment or ignorance, where the very vividness or intensity of the images of the mind's lucidity overpowers the mind.

Question: Would you explain more about superimposition and denial?
Rinpoche: Superimposition, or exaggeration, is the mistaken belief that something exists when it actually does not exist. To give an example, we could have the belief that all appearances are truly existent. In reality,

however, they are not truly existent but empty, although to a confused person they seem real. In terms of direct cognition, superimposition is when we look at the mind and make the mistake of believing thoughts and emotions are real.

The other mistake, denial, occurs when we believe that what actually exists does not exist. In the context of inference, we may decide that emptiness is not the ultimate truth. In the context of direct experience, we may fail to recognize the mind's nature as being the unity of emptiness and cognitive lucidity.

Path Mahāmudrā 4

WE NEED TO ENTER A PATH, and having entered it, we should reach the end of the path and attain its fruition. Just entering the path is not enough, and to reach its result, we have to make sure that we enter the path correctly and avoid mistaken ways. In this section, the path of mahāmudrā is presented in two sections: discarding attachment to mistaken paths and finding the authentic path of mahāmudrā. The first part of the teaching, discarding attachment to mistaken paths, has eight sections.

Discarding Attachment to Mistaken Paths

ATTACHMENT TO KARMAMUDRĀ

21. Once totally attached to kissing and the bliss of what follows,
     The ignorant say that this is indeed the ultimate.
     Having left his house, he stands in front of the gate,
     Soliciting tales of sensual pleasure.

Verse 21 may seem like a general criticism of the path of method. However, Saraha is not saying that the path of method is ineffective and will not lead to the fruition; what he intends here is that if the path of method is not accompanied by recognition of the mind's nature, it is not effective. Pursuing the path of method without the path of liberation, which leads to the recognition of mind's nature, you will not find ultimate freedom and omniscience. And conversely, if the path of method is accompanied by the recognition of the mind's nature, you will come to fruition.

There is a difference between the path of method and the path of liberation in terms of recognizing the nature of mind. How is this so? The most effective way to practice the path is to integrate the path of liberation with the path of method. If that is not possible, we can practice the path of liberation alone and it will still be a good and effective path. It will lead to abandoning what should be abandoned and realizing what should be realized, and therefore it will bring about the fruition of the path. On the other hand, practicing the path of method in the complete absence of the path of liberation will not lead to any significant or worthy result.

In verse 21 Saraha specifically criticizes the view that the practice of karmamudrā[40] without the wisdom of mahāmudrā will lead to awakening. The analogy is the following. If you are in your house, you can enjoy all the good things that you have inside; however, if you sit outside your house, refusing to go inside and merely talking about the good things that are there, you cannot actually enjoy them. In the same way, when you attempt to practice the path of method without the path of liberation, you are like the person who is sitting outside his or her house and unable to enjoy all the things you describe. In sum, this verse is a criticism of the practice of karmamudrā in isolation from the wisdom of mahāmudrā.

ATTACHMENT TO THE SUBTLE BODY

22. For the sake of the winds, you meditate on your body as an
        empty house,
     Practicing artificial methods in great variety and number.

From space it falls, along with faults.[41]
Overwhelmed, the yogi faints away.

Verse 22 criticizes the attempt to practice with the subtle channels, winds, and drops without engaging in the path of liberation or mahāmudrā. The type of practice that Saraha refers to here is manipulating our subtle channels, winds, and drops[42] to bring about various experiences. You can derive benefit from this practice, because it can enhance your experience of the mind's nature. But if there is no practice of mahāmudrā—and therefore no experience of the mind's nature to begin with—simply working with the subtle channels, winds, and drops in isolation will not produce any significant result. Not only that, these practices may actually be very dangerous. The verse states: "Overwhelmed, the yogi faints away."

In *A Song for the King*, there is a clear emphasis on the path of liberation. It is important to understand that it is not that the path of method is invalid or useless, but for it to be effective, it must be accompanied by the path of liberation, which is more important. This stanza is not so different from the previous stanzas that dealt with not relying solely on the conceptual certainty derived from the logical reasoning and the wisdom born of hearing or reflection. Of greater importance than conceptual certainty is direct realization, which arises from meditation. In the same way, the practice of mahāmudrā is more important than the practice of the methods of karmamudrā or the channels, winds, and drops.

In short, what really matters is recognition of the nature of our mind. If this recognition is present and the path of method is not practiced, you can still be liberated. If this recognition is absent, then no matter how much you practice, the path of method will not bring liberation.

ATTACHMENT TO PASSING EXPERIENCES

23.   Just as Brahmins make their burnt offerings
       Of ghee and rice in a blazing fire,
       Know that, from *Ham*, the quintessence of space, the substance
          of nectar produces experience;
       The passing experience of bliss is grasped as reality.

The third instruction concerning what to avoid is not to become attached to minor experiences. There are two parts to this verse. The analogy is given in the first two lines and the meaning in the second two. The Brahmins' burnt offerings are an analogy for the incorrect practice of the path of method. It is the custom of Brahmins to make fire offerings without cultivating samādhi or performing any kind of visualization. Proud of being the highest caste in Indian society, they simply assume that igniting these substances and saying the ritual words will be of benefit so they burn substances such as ghee and rice to make offerings to the gods.

   If the practice of burnt offerings is accompanied by one-pointed concentration *(samādhi)* and visualization, it can be useful. But if it is just setting food ablaze, it will not lead to anything. The offerings do get burned up, but aside from that, there is no other real result.

   This example can also refer to practicing the path of method without any realization of emptiness. If we practice the path of method, then through the power of the techniques themselves, we can indeed cause the nectar to descend from the essence of space or the *Ham* syllable within our head. If we are successful, we will experience physical bliss. But if this practice is not conjoined with meditation on emptiness, it cannot possibly lead to the final result—realizing the unity of bliss and emptiness. The drops will descend and you will feel very good for a while, but that is it. Nothing else will come of it because an important aspect of the practice is missing. So the point here is that to practice the path of method without realizing emptiness is of no greater significance than simply throwing food into fire and thinking that this is a grand offering.

The verse emphasizes the importance of generating authentic experience and realization. To avoid a possible misunderstanding, it is crucial to know what this verse does and does not say. As we have seen, our path consists of gathering the two accumulations of merit and wisdom, which assist one another. For example, on the path of a bodhisattva, the first five of the six perfections—generosity, morality, patience, diligence, and meditation—enable the development of the sixth, the perfection of intelligence or wisdom. Because these perfections are joined with wisdom, they become pure and transcendent. We should not think, therefore, that this verse says that the practices involving conceptualization are to be utterly dismissed. We do make offerings to the Three Jewels, give generously to the needy, maintain moral discipline, cultivate patience, and so on. All of these practices are important branches of the conceptual accumulation of merit. Our practice does not consist only of meditation on the mind's nature in isolation from anything else.

We might incorrectly think that the great Brahmin Saraha has taught that all conceptual practices are utterly useless. That would be a misunderstanding. These practices are actually very useful. But the point of practicing the perfections is the realization of mahāmudrā. The great Śāntideva in *A Guide to the Bodhisattva's Way of Life* writes: "These five branches were taught by the Buddha for the sake of wisdom." In other words, we cultivate the conceptual accumulation of merit to realize mahāmudrā, to achieve the nonconceptual accumulation of wisdom. In fact, consciously cultivating the conceptual accumulation of merit is necessary to develop wisdom. But while we are accumulating this merit, we must join it with the nonconceptual accumulation of wisdom. Otherwise, Śāntideva says, "In the absence of wisdom, the other five virtues do not become perfections because they lack the perfection of wisdom."

So this verse points out that while it is valuable to perform practices, such as burnt offerings, on the path of method, they should always be conjoined with mahāmudrā experience.

In the *Collected Sutras*,[43] the following analogy is presented by the Buddha: "If sightless people were gathered together in an empty valley and tried to find their way into town, they would not be able to discover it and would wander around aimlessly. But if one person with sight were to accompany them, they could easily reach the town." In the same way, like sightless people, the five perfections on their own are limited; they can lead only to temporary well-being and prosperity, but not to full awakening. But just as one person with sight can lead a large crowd of blind people to their destination, the sixth perfection joined with the other five causes them to become an effective means for the achievement of enlightenment. In the same way, the great Brahmin Saraha indicates that these practices alone will not lead to awakening unless they are joined with the practice of mahāmudrā.

Many of us have experienced this in our practice. Students have come to me and said that they are very interested in and devoted to the practice of meditation, that they are diligent and really trying, but do not seem to be making progress and have become dissatisfied. When they say there is no improvement, the reason may be that their meditation needs to be supplemented with the accumulation of merit. For example, in the context of Vajrayāna practice, guru yoga and supplication are the basis for meditation. With our body, we can perform prostrations and circumambulation to accumulate merit. With our speech, we can do liturgical practice and mantra repetition. With our mind, we can meditate on compassion. With our wealth we can engage in acts of generosity.

All of these activities will help our meditation practice to progress. Since these virtuous deeds are combined with the practice of meditation, they will not just lead to a temporary benefit, which occurs with most ordinary acts of defiled virtue,[44] but help us to move along the path to awakening.

In sum, Saraha is not saying that the path of means or the accumulation of merit is not useful. Rather, he is demonstrating its validity by showing that it must be combined with the realization of mahāmudrā.

THE INCORRECT PRACTICE OF INNER HEAT

24. Some make the firelight burn and bring it to their fontanel;
    With their tongue they enjoy union with the smaller one.
    This binds them up and makes them thoroughly disturbed.
    Swayed by pride, they call themselves yogis.

Here, Saraha describes the incorrect practice of inner heat that is more characteristic of non-Buddhist traditions. This physical technique creates the blazing of fire from the abdomen, which causes the subtle drops to descend from the top of one's head and land on one's tongue, producing a state of great pleasure.[45] However, if this is not motivated by the wish to realize mahāmudrā and not combined with its practice, the experience of the pleasure of inner heat alone will only lead to attachment to that bliss.

Meditation practice should create something more than mere attachment to such experiences, and the verse describes the negative result of such techniques: The practitioners become thoroughly disturbed and obsessed with an attachment, which they have created for this experience. Not only do they become obsessed, they also develop pride, because they think that their experience is very special and that it allows them to call themselves yogis. But without recognizing their mind's nature, they are unfit to be called yogis and have nothing to be proud of.

MISTAKING SELF-AWARENESS

25. An experience of self-awareness, a mere name, they display with a
        proud intellect.
     "Whatever binds, that itself liberates," so they say.
     Not knowing how to appraise a gem, the ignorant
     Single out the color green to say that some trinket is an emerald.

This verse addresses the topic of self-awareness.[46] The term is used in
several different contexts in Buddhism. In the study of valid cognition
and in some Middle Way school contexts, it is said that self-awareness
exists, meaning that one can know what one is experiencing. In other
presentations of the Middle Way, it is said that self-awareness is impos-
sible: the mind being aware of itself resembles a sword being able to cut
itself or a strong man being able to lift himself. But in mahāmudrā and
similar teachings, the term *self-awareness* means something else. It refers
to self-aware wisdom[47] that is nondual. So we seem to have three con-
texts for this term; first, that of valid cognition, where essentially self-
awareness seems to be a relative truth; second, where it appears to be
refuted as an ultimate truth; and third, in the teachings of mahāmudrā,
where it is asserted to be the pinnacle of the view. At first glance these
three presentations may seem to be in conflict, but in fact they are not.

For example, when we are practicing tranquility meditation, culti-
vating mindfulness and alertness, at some point we become aware that
our mind is at rest. This awareness is merely awareness of what our mind
is experiencing at that moment. This is a valid experience for tranquil-
ity meditation, but in itself, it is not of much use in the practice of
insight meditation.

The self-aware wisdom that is sought in the practice of insight is dif-
ferent. It is not merely the mind's ability to know what it is experienc-
ing; rather, it is the mind actually recognizing and directly experiencing

its own nature. Now that nature, as mentioned earlier, is emptiness, but it is not just emptiness, because the mind also has the ability to cognize. So the experience is of the unity of cognitive lucidity and emptiness, which is sometimes called the unity of expanse and wisdom. This recognition and experience is entirely different from the mind being aware of what it is experiencing, such as being at rest or moving.

The self-awareness in terms of valid cognition is simply the capacity of any cognition to experience itself in the most basic sense. According to valid cognition, each of the eight consciousnesses (the five sensory consciousnesses, the mental consciousness, the afflicted consciousness, and the ālaya consciousness) has this ability to be self-aware, which is simply the fact that a consciousness is not concealed from itself. For example, this means that you know what has arisen in your mind without having to ask anyone else or without having to deduce it; you just experience it. This is what self-awareness means in the basic context of valid cognition. You know what you see with your eye consciousness. However, you do not know what arises in the minds of others or what they see, so you have to ask them what they are thinking. By contrast, you know what is in your own mind without having to ask yourself what you are thinking, and you do not need to follow a process of deduction to figure it out. This self-awareness is on the mundane level, meaning that it is limited to the world of relative truth. This is not the self-aware wisdom spoken of in mahāmudrā.

The Middle Way school's presentation of self-awareness is given, for example, in Candrakīrti's *Entering the Middle Way* and Śāntideva's *Guide to the Bodhisattva's Way of Life*, both of which contain refutations of self-awareness. But the self-awareness refuted in these texts is one that cannot possibly exist. Further, it is not the self-awareness described in texts on valid cognition, nor is it the self-aware wisdom discussed in the mahāmudrā teachings. What is refuted in the Middle Way school is self-awareness in the sense of the mind being able to see itself as an object that is other to itself. This argument negates a self-awareness that would arise from having the duality of a separate subject and object. This kind of self-awareness is refuted using analogies such as the impossibility of a sword cutting itself.

Now this is very different from the self-aware wisdom of mahāmudrā that is free of subject and object. This self-aware wisdom of mahāmudrā is not the mind seeing itself as an object of perception that would be a solid or substantial thing. In the practice of cutting through the ego (Tib. *chö*) we say, "Homage to the Great Mother Prajñāpāramitā, who is the experience of self-aware wisdom." This means that self-aware wisdom occurs when the mind sees its own primordial freedom from samsaric or substantial existence: the mind sees its own nature, which from the very beginning is free. This freedom from existence is not a nothingness or a voidness, because cognitive lucidity is present at the same time. Since mind's nature has this inherent wisdom, it can cognize and therefore it can cognize itself. In that this nature knows itself, it is without the duality of viewer and viewed. This is the self-awareness spoken of in mahāmudrā.

The verse describes the situation of someone who has an experience of self-awareness and taking it to be self-aware wisdom recognizing the true nature of the mind, proudly explains this experience to others. It could have been an experience of ordinary self-awareness on the level of relative truth as described in valid cognition, or it could be a mistaken view of the existence of self-awareness that is refuted in the Middle Way school. In either case, it is not the true experience of self-aware wisdom. Making the mistake of taking simple awareness of your mind for the experience of the mind's nature leads you to assume that this alone will liberate you. When speaking to others you might say, "Whatever binds, that itself liberates."

The distinction the practitioner fails to make is that the self-aware wisdom described in mahāmudrā is not merely the experience of the mind as it normally is. It is the recognition of the mind's true nature. The simple experience of the mind is the self-awareness described in valid cognition. But the recognition of the mind's nature is seeing or experiencing the mind's emptiness and at the same time, experiencing the mind's cognitive lucidity, inseparable from that emptiness. Self-aware wisdom is the wisdom of the direct experience of emptiness and lucidity. Experiencing the unity of emptiness and lucidity will liberate you, but merely being aware of your mind will not.

The analogy for mistaking mere self-awareness for self-aware wisdom is mistaking a green trinket for an emerald. What they have in common is the color green, just as what self-awareness and self-aware wisdom have in common is self-awareness. Aside from the color, there is a great difference between a trinket and an emerald. Mistaking one for the other simply means that you do not know what the characteristics of an emerald are. In the same way, when you mistake self-awareness for self-aware wisdom, it means that you do not know what the characteristics of self-aware wisdom are.

MISTAKING PASSING EXPERIENCE FOR REALIZATION

26. This is bringing brass to mind as gold.
     You think carrying this experience onto the path will accomplish
        the ultimate.
     That is like being attached to the bliss of a dream.
     You claim that the aggregates are impermanent and bliss is
        permanent?

This verse is concerned with attachment to minor or temporary experiences. The analogy presented here is the mistaking of brass for gold, which resembles the previous analogy of mistaking a green trinket for an emerald because of their similar color. In the same way, you might mistake brass for gold. If you have recognized gold as gold, it is very beneficial. But if you mistake brass for gold, you merely become confused. When you are practicing meditation, if you mistake a temporary experience for a state of attainment, you are deceived in a similar way. Just as brass does not have the value of gold, temporary experiences do not have the value of true realization.

It is normal and healthy for temporary experiences to arise from time to time, whether you are practicing tranquility or insight meditation. But these experiences have no great value in and of themselves. Therefore it is said, "Temporary experiences are like mist; they will vanish." It is also said, "If you have become attached to positive experiences, such as bliss, lucidity, and nonconceptuality, you lack the view." Experiences can sometimes be very positive, like the three just mentioned. But if you are caught by these passing experiences and think they should be maintained, you have lost the view. Why? Because having these experiences is not the purpose of meditation. The point of meditation is to recognize the nature of the mind. Therefore, the second line of this verse states that holding on to such experiences will not help you, because you cannot accomplish the ultimate aim of meditation.

For example, when Gampopa was studying under the supervision of Milarepa, he had many different experiences and visions because he was working with the subtle channels and winds. Sometimes Gampopa saw the mandalas of various deities before him; at other times the place where he was practicing seemed to be engulfed in utter darkness. Gampopa thought, "Since my guru is like the Buddha, I must surely ask him about my experiences, both the good and the bad ones." Also during this time Gampopa was having a lot of very strange and vivid dreams. When he asked Milarepa about them, Milarepa replied, "You are a great teacher of the Kadampa and you must have heard and studied the Buddha's teachings extensively. Do you not remember that the Buddha said that dreams are merely illusions, that in fact dreams exemplify the state of illusion?

Was the Buddha joking when he said this?" Milarepa went on to explain, "When we meditate, many new experiences arise in our mind, because we are working with our mind in a new way. There is no reason to be elated by pleasant experiences or depressed by unpleasant ones."

Then Milarepa gave an example: if you are looking at the moon and press your eyes with your fingers, you will see two moons. Seeing this, some might think, "Well, most people see one moon and I see two moons, so I must be special," and so they develop a sense of pride. But there is no reason to be proud of simply pressing your eyes with your fingers. Upon seeing two moons others might think, "Most people see one moon and I see two, so there must be something terribly wrong with me." But in fact, there is nothing wrong; you were just pressing your eyes. This is the analogy that Milarepa used to explain how we should relate to the experiences in meditation.

This verse gives a second analogy for attachment to temporary meditation experiences by comparing them to a dream. If we are attached to something in a dream, it obviously is not going to last, because the dream state is so impermanent. You could say that the pleasure experienced in a dream has even less value, because it is even shorter and less stable than the pleasure experienced in the waking state. Further, the state of dreaming is one of added confusion, because these images in a dream come from the confused images of phenomena we experience in our waking life. It is, therefore, of no use to try to hold on to something that happened in a dream. In the same way, when we practice meditation, various experiences will arise and it is important not to fixate on them or become attached.

For example, a positive experience might occur in our meditation. Afterward, we reflect upon it and think, "I had a good experience." But in thinking of it as a good experience, we create the desire for this temporary experience to reoccur. If the next day during practice it does not reoccur, we are automatically disappointed. There is nothing wrong with the experience, which is good, but it is simply an indication that we are practicing. We should not try to prolong it or to hope that it will reoccur, because it has no value in and of itself. When an experience arises, simply continue to practice meditation as before. If an experience stops arising, just continue to practice meditation as before. Becoming attached to any type of meditation—experiences, visions, dreams, whatever—will bind you. Do not regard these things as having any particular positive or negative value or judge them as good or bad. They are just appearances within the mind, which do not justify desire or fear.

Having the expectation that the meditation experience will last is setting yourself up for disappointment, or as it says in the fourth line: "You claim that the aggregates are impermanent and bliss is permanent?" In other words, you know that the aggregates are impermanent and yet you expect the bliss experienced by these impermanent aggregates to be permanent and outlast them. The meditative state that produces the particular experience is impermanent, and therefore the experience is impermanent. In the same way, you cannot expect the product of meditation—a state of bliss that is grounded in a certain set of aggregates—to outlast those very aggregates, which are changing moment to moment.

ABANDONING CONFUSION ABOUT E VAM

27. The letters *E Vam* make themselves understood.[48]
     By classifying four moments, the four seals are set out.
     Some claim that through experiences, spontaneous presence
         appears.
     Do not be like the one attached to the mirror's reflection.

The seventh mistake is to become attached to spontaneous presence. This is expressed in symbolic terms, which are particular to the Vajrayāna and which explain the unity of emptiness and wisdom, or the unity of wisdom and method. The symbol for this unity is the word *E Vam: E* represents emptiness and the unborn expanse, while *Vam* represents wisdom and also method. Together these two represent the true nature, which is, on the one hand, emptiness and, on the other hand, spontaneously present, luminous clarity. The mistaken path pointed out in this verse is thinking that the experience of doing the practice of the subtle channels, winds, and drops by itself is the ultimate *E Vam*. These practices are important and helpful for the ultimate realization of mahāmudrā. However, as explained earlier in the text, if these methods are not combined with the realization of mahāmudrā, or if we become attached to the experience of these methods, they become an obstacle to achieving enlightenment.

Verse 27 mentions the four seals or mudrās. To understand what Saraha is going to say about the four seals, we need to understand a set of four symbols and another set of four seals. The four symbols are aspects or stages of the practice and the realization of mahāmudrā. They are unique to Saraha's presentation of mahāmudrā in his cycle of three songs, to which *A Song for the King* belongs. The four symbols are: mindfulness, nonminding, the unborn, and beyond the intellect.

The first symbol is mindfulness, which refers to the proper cultivation of the faculty of mindfulness, or recollection, and its attendant faculty of alertness, which reins in distraction.[49] This is practiced as a method for pacifying the mind. Here, however, it does not just refer to tranquility meditation, because it also includes certainty about the illusory nature of phenomenon. This will be explained in detail later.

The second symbol is nonminding. Through the practice of mindfulness and alertness, the mind has come to rest, and then we go beyond this mere resting. Due to the heightening of the mind's innate cognitive lucidity, the mind is able to recognize the emptiness of mindfulness itself.[50]

Through this realization, we achieve the third symbol, which is the unborn. This aspect is the recognition that all dharmas are empty and therefore are without any true arising—they are unborn. Finally, when realizing this third symbol, we achieve the fourth symbol, which is to experience directly the dharmadhātu (the expanse of all phenomena), completely free of any intellectual contrivance or fabrication. This fourth symbol is therefore called beyond the intellect.

These four symbols can be correlated with the four joys and the four seals. The four seals are explained in this verse in two ways. The first way shows how they should be known in a correct understanding of ultimate truth. Then, indicating a second way, Saraha will return to them and criticize a misunderstanding of the four seals.

To correlate these four symbols with the four joys, we begin with an ordinary state that lacks mindfulness and alertness; for this reason, we are afflicted by the disturbing emotions. This is a state of misery. Then, through the instructions of the guru, we reach the first stage of mindfulness, pacifying our mind and realizing the illusory nature of phenomena. This experience results in the joy of the first stage. When we have reached the second stage, nonminding, we realize that both mindfulness and the nature of mind are empty. The experience of this freedom brings about a second kind of joy, known as supreme joy, which is stronger than the first.

When we reach the third stage, the unborn, we see that mindfulness, nonminding, and indeed all phenomena are unborn. This produces a much greater joy known as without joy, which means a joy so great that there is no longer any attachment to it. Finally, when we realize that mindfulness, nonminding, and the unborn nature can only be realized in a state beyond the intellect (Saraha's fourth symbol), then the experience of the fourth joy arises, which is known as coemergent joy. If the practices of the subtle winds and channels are done without the recognition of the mind's nature, one will experience these four joys as mere physical sensations.

Now we can correlate these four joys and the four symbols, or stages, of Saraha with the four seals. At the first stage of mindfulness, we see all relative truths or phenomena as they are and experience the first joy. This results in the first seal, the dharma-mudrā, or seal of dharmas, which mean "phenomena" in this context. At the second stage, non-minding, which is also supreme joy, we see the emptiness of mind's nature. This is the jñāna-mudrā, or wisdom seal. In the third stage, the unborn, we see that both mindfulness and nonminding are unborn and thereby achieve the joy that is without attachment to joy. This is the samaya-mudrā, or commitment seal. And finally, when we realize that all these previous three stages are by nature beyond the intellect, we achieve coemergent joy. This is the mahā-mudrā, or the great seal. Here, the term *seal* is understood as the correct realization of ultimate truth. Saraha affirms that one needs to realize these four joys and four seals, which are the true meaning of *E Vam*.

It is important to note that these terms, particularly the four joys and the four seals, are also applied to the physical and mental sensations that arise during the practices of the subtle channels, winds, and drops. The physical and cognitive sensations experienced at this time are also called joy, supreme joy, without joy, and coemergent joy. And sometimes the terminology of the four seals—the dharma seal, the wisdom seal, the samaya seal, and the great seal—are applied to results of these practices of the path of method.

Saraha criticizes the use of this terminology when it is applied merely to the sensations that arise from the practices of the channels, winds, and drops. If we assume that we have experienced the fourth joy and thereby conclude we have realized coemergent wisdom, we are mistaken. If we actually do succeed in realizing coemergent wisdom through the practices of the subtle channels, winds, and drops, that, of course, is fine and these practices have assumed their proper function. But the simple experience of the sensation of these four joys alone does not constitute the realization of coemergent wisdom. Saraha states that confusing the mere experience of the sensation of what is commonly called coemergent joy with the true realization of coemergent wisdom is like confusing the mere reflection in a mirror for the real thing: "Do not be like the one attached to the mirror's reflection." As before, Saraha is not arguing about the validity of using the subtle channels, winds, and drops as methods. But he is saying that if they are not used to bring realization of mahāmudrā, then all that they lead to is something that does not really perform any true function or have any true value.

This completes the first seven of the eight verses concerned with pointing out mistaken paths. These seven verses are mainly criticizing two things. One is the mistaken perception that the path of method alone is sufficient to bring about realization of the ultimate. The other is becoming attached to the wisdom of hearing and reflection. The problem with these two mistakes is that they prevent us from entering the authentic path. So attachment to the wisdom of hearing and reflection or to the experience arising from the techniques on the path of method can be an obstacle. This is not to say that the wisdom of hearing and reflection or the experience of the path of method are themselves obstacles. The wisdom of hearing and reflection can be very helpful, but if you become attached to them, they become an impediment. In both cases of attachment to wisdom or method, we are prevented from realizing ultimate truth.

MISTAKING THE RELATIVE TRUTH

28.   Not understanding, the deer runs
      In confusion after the water's mirage.
      Likewise, the ignorant cannot evade thirst, and die.
      Claiming it is ultimate, some take up bliss.

This verse summarizes what is wrong with a mistaken path by using the analogy of a deer chasing after a mirage of water. The deer seeks to quench its thirst but misapprehends the shimmering mirage for water. The deer's thirst, of course, is not relieved, and it remains dissatisfied and suffering additionally from its disappointment. In the same way, if we become attached to the path of means or the wisdom of hearing and reflection as ends in themselves, we prevent them from serving their true function, which is to lead us toward the realization of ultimate truth. Like the deer that remains thirsty, we remain in suffering and do not find true realization. Therefore, it says in the fourth line of the verse: "Claiming it is ultimate, some take up bliss." Thinking that the experience of the bliss, the pleasure of the path of method, is ultimate, they become attached to it.

Gampopa, whose tradition we follow, said that we should combine hearing, reflection, and meditation. This means that we should combine our study with the practice of mahāmudrā meditation, both during meditation sessions and in postmeditation. In this way, our understanding is not divorced from practical experience.

In the same way, we engage in both practices of the path of means: the generation stage of yidam practice and the completion stage. These are very important and useful, but they need to be practiced in a way that is not divorced from the mahāmudrā experience of the mind's nature. Even in postmeditation, we need to combine everything with the practice of mahāmudrā, whether we are engaging in physical acts of virtue, such as prostration and circumambulation, or in verbal acts such as liturgical practice and mantra repetition, or in mental acts such as the cultivation of love and compassion for others. To practice all the techniques of the path of method together with mahāmudrā is best. If not, at least we should try to practice in a way that is not devoid of mahāmudrā experience. In that way we avoid the eight errors that Saraha has pointed out in these eight verses and become capable of pursuing an authentic path.

The Authentic Path of Mahāmudrā

THE FOUR SYMBOLS IN BRIEF

29. The relative truth refers to mindfulness; nonminding
     Points to those mental states when the mind is released from
        mindfulness.
     When completely transformed, this is the supreme of the supreme.
     The result is the genuine supreme. Friends, you should know these.

With this verse Saraha begins the second part of the path of mahāmudrā,
which is the presentation of the genuine path. As mentioned earlier, his
cycle of three songs presents the authentic path using the unique set of
terms called the four symbols of instruction. An overview of these four
symbols is given in verse 29.

The first symbol is mindfulness, or recollection. When we start to
practice, our mind is filled with thoughts, which disturb it like waves on
the surface of water. The Third Karmapa, Rangjung Dorjé, in his *Aspi-
ration Prayer of Mahāmudrā,* wrote: "May the waves of coarse and subtle
thoughts be pacified in their own place, and may the river of mind come
to rest without movement." How do we pacify these waves of thought?
How do we bring our mind to rest? We do this through the application
of two faculties of the mind: mindfulness and alertness. When mindful-
ness is active and keeping the mind directed toward the focus of medita-
tion, alertness will automatically be present and signaling when the mind
strays. By the same token, when one loses mindfulness, alertness disap-
pears. So the single most important thing in the beginning of meditation
practice is mindfulness. To emphasize this, Śāntideva wrote in *A Guide to
the Bodhisattva's Way of Life:* "With joined palms I pray to all practition-
ers to rely upon mindfulness, which alone can calm the wild mind." Here,
in this practice, we are mainly recollecting the illusory nature of phe-
nomena; therefore, it is a recollection of relative truth.

The second symbol is nonminding. Through the practice of mindfulness, we develop a state of mental stability and stillness. This is merely a state of tranquility and not the recognition of the mind's true nature. Therefore, we need to go further and practice the second symbol, which is nonminding. This does not mean that we lose the faculty of mindfulness; rather, it means seeing the nature of the mind, seeing the emptiness of even mindfulness itself. This is referred to in Rangjung Dorjé's *Aspiration Prayer of Mahāmudrā:* "By looking again and again at the nature of mind which cannot be looked at, one clearly sees the meaning of what cannot be seen." So the second symbol is the samādhi of insight, or insight meditation. This second symbol arises when thoughts have been pacified through mindfulness and we begin to see the mind's nature beyond elaboration.

This awareness is expanded further until we not only recognize the nature of our mind but also recognize this nature to be the true nature of all phenomena. In short, we see that they are all unborn and without true arising. This is the third symbol. In the verse it states, "When completely transformed, this is the supreme of the supreme." Previously, we had recognized the mind as beyond elaboration, and now "the supreme of the supreme" refers to the time when that realization becomes so vast in scope that it is all-pervasive. We realize directly that this unborn quality is not limited to the nature of mind but belongs to the nature of all phenomena. This is how we recognize that all phenomena are unborn, which leads in turn to the fourth symbol, beyond the intellect. This is referred to in the fourth line, which states, "The result is the genuine supreme." The genuine supreme is the complete realization, beyond the intellect, of the nature of all phenomena. It is these four symbols of the authentic path that Saraha says we should know: mindfulness, nonminding, the unborn, and beyond the intellect.

THE SYMBOLS, JOYS, SEALS, AND SAMĀDHIS

	1	2	3	4
Saraha's Four Symbols	mindfulness	nonminding	the unborn	beyond the intellect
The Four Joys	joy	supreme joy	without joy	coemergent joy
The Four Seals (Mudrā)	Dharma seal	wisdom seal	samaya seal	great seal
The Four Samādhis	samādhi of illusion-like phenomena	samādhi of the lion's play	heroic samādhi	vajralike samādhi

In a more detailed explanation of his four symbols, Saraha identifies them with the four one-pointed meditative concentrations or samādhis described by the Buddha in the sutras. (See table above.) The four samādhis are the samādhi of illusion-like phenomena, the samādhi of the lion's play, the heroic samādhi, and the vajralike samādhi. The first, the samādhi of illusion-like phenomena, refers to the first stage of mindfulness, which is seeing the illusory nature of relative truth. The second symbol is nonminding. At that point, we further see that relative appearances have no true existence, that they are mere play or display. In this way, we achieve the samādhi of the lion's play. The third symbol, the unborn, is the achievement of the state beyond fear, because we recognize the unborn nature of all things, and therefore it is the culmination of the heroic samādhi. And the fourth symbol, the realization of that which is beyond the intellect, is indestructible realization; it is therefore the result of vajralike samādhi. This concludes a brief explanation of how the four symbols are related to the four samādhis.[51]

In the next four verses, Saraha will explain these four samādhis in detail. However, when he does so, he does not follow the order that he has previously used (mindfulness, nonminding, the unborn, and beyond the intellect). Instead Saraha starts with nonminding, then returns to mindfulness, followed by the unborn, and finally, beyond the intellect.

It could be that he presents nonminding in the beginning so that we do not merely cultivate a state of tranquility meditation. Before beginning the proper practice of mindfulness, we have become somewhat familiar with the mind's nature through the presentation of nonminding. Having gained a sense of what it is, we are able to stabilize this through the subsequent practice of mindfulness.

The Second Symbol: Nonminding

30. The mind released from mindfulness engages in samādhi.
     It is completely purified of the afflictions.
     As the utpala born from a swamp is not stained by it,
     So the mind itself is not affected by the faults arising from
         samsara nor by the qualities found in the Victorious One.

In verse 30, Saraha presents the practice of nonminding, which is identified with the samādhi of the lion's play. When we begin to practice tranquility on the path of mahāmudrā, we start with the recognition of the mind's nature. Because of this, the practice of meditation is not devoid of wisdom; from the very beginning, it is endowed with the wisdom that comes from meditation. Nonminding resembles the behavior or play of a lion, because just as a lion terrifies and overpowers all other wild animals, nonminding (meaning here the recognition of the mind's nature) overpowers and defeats all mental afflictions.

In the first line, "The mind released from mindfulness engages in samādhi," Saraha affirms that we begin with the faculty of mindfulness. We are released from it because we have recognized the nature of mind, which brings freedom from the disturbing emotions. The mind is completely purified. This does not mean, however, that one solid thing is overpowering another solid thing. Nonminding is a deep insight into the nonexistence of the disturbing emotions, and this is what conquers them. In the next two lines, Saraha gives an analogy to illustrate this meaning: "As the utpala born from a swamp is not stained by it, so the mind itself is not affected by the faults arising from samsara nor by the qualities found in the Victorious One." The utpala is a blue lotus flower, which grows in the mud. In sustaining its purity, regardless of the nature of its environment, the utpala resembles nonminding or insight into the nature of mind.

THE FIRST SYMBOL: THE PRACTICE OF MINDFULNESS

31. Mindfulness also sees with certainty that all things are like an illusion.
Transcending the world, take this moment into your mind and rest evenly in meditation.
Those whose minds recognize the teaching bind up ignorance.
Self-arising and inconceivable, wisdom naturally abides within.

As we saw in the brief presentation, nonminding is presented first and mindfulness second, because even though we have gained some insight into the mind's nature, that experience cannot simply be left as it is or abandoned; it has to be cultivated. Dakpo Tashi Namgyal wrote, "The cultivation of this insight requires sharp and lucid mindfulness and alertness." After initially recognizing the mind's nature, which is beyond mindfulness, we still need to apply the faculty of mindfulness to stabilize that recognition. This is probably the reason Saraha has presented nonminding first and then the practice of mindfulness. Due to this change in order, the faculty of mindfulness here is different. Since it succeeds the recognition of nonminding, it is free of fixation and therefore sees the illusory nature of things. The first line of the verse states: "Mindfulness also sees with certainty that all things are like an illusion." Of the four types of samādhi, it is the first, the samādhi of illusion-like phenomena, that is relevant here.

Having recognized the nature of the mind, or mahāmudrā, we must take the next step and stabilize that state of recognition. Progress in the practice depends upon cultivating faculties of mindfulness and alertness, which are lucid and sharp. If we do not maintain them, or if they are not intense enough, we will not be able to cut through the undercurrent of our thoughts. This undercurrent refers to thoughts that are not superficially evident but can persist unnoticed and adulterate our meditation. Furthermore, if we get used to allowing these conceptual undercurrents to continue, our samādhi will eventually become defective and this will prevent progress. Maintaining lucid and sharp mindfulness and alertness allows for greater progress.

The reason the practice of mindfulness is correlated with the samādhi of illusion-like phenomena is that through practicing nonminding, we have recognized the mind's nature. Since this is a basic recognition of dharmatā, there is no fixation on the reality of the meditative state or the faculty of mindfulness that is being cultivated. It is all seen as a magical illusion.

THE THIRD SYMBOL: THE UNBORN

32. These empty appearances have the nature of clarity; from the
      very first they are unborn.
    They do not arise as an entity with form; discard as well thinking
      they arise in the aspect of form's characteristics.
    Abide continually within the mind itself and practice only deep
      meditation.
    Without thought, rest in this meditation free of mental activity
      and free of flaws.

The practice of the third symbol, the unborn, is mainly a meditation on emptiness. This is a high level of experience and realization, but it is not the ultimate realization. For example, followers of the Middle Way school study what it means to be empty of self, and this is similar to the realization of the unborn. This is followed by the study of what it means to be empty of other, or the emptiness of phenomena. It explains that emptiness is not just empty; emptiness is also the spontaneous presence of wisdom within each and every being. The emptiness of phenomena and the spontaneous presence of wisdom may seem like very high teachings, and therefore very distant from our ordinary experience. In mahāmudrā meditation, however, this same sugatagarbha, the seed of enlightenment, is presented in such a way that it does not seem distant from our ordinary experience. Sugatagarbha is the mind's cognitive lucidity, or the mind's innate wisdom, and the seed of all the qualities of buddhahood.

Through the practice of mindfulness and nonminding, we come to realize the third symbol, the unborn. This is the realization that all appearances from the very beginning have been without birth or true arising. It is traditionally said that mahāmudrā realization is devoid of the three conditions and beyond the four joys.[52] "Without the three conditions" means that mahāmudrā meditation is independent of the three experiences of bliss, cognitive lucidity, and nonconceptuality. Whereas most meditative states are dependent upon one or more of these, mahāmudrā is not. While most other meditative states are considered conditioned, mahāmudrā is not. Therefore, mahāmudrā is unborn from the beginning, and so it neither abides nor ceases.

Furthermore, in referring to empty appearances, the second line states, "They do not arise as an entity with form; discard as well thinking they arise in the aspect of form's characteristics." Mahāmudrā has no form. When you look directly at your mind, you do not detect any shape or color. This means that the mind's nature has no form, and further, that it does not possess any of the characteristics of form or solidity either. In this way mahāmudrā is shown to be unborn.

What exactly is the unborn nature of phenomena? While in ultimate truth nothing truly exists, in relative truth various appearances do arise. If we examine these appearances, we will see that their nature is the unity of emptiness and appearance. The same is true of experiences within the mind, such as meditative states of bliss. If we look at the nature of bliss, we will see that it is empty. Since we are experiencing bliss, this is the unity of bliss and emptiness. Furthermore, the capacity to recognize, to know, or to be aware is characteristic of the unborn mind. If we look at this awareness and see its emptiness, that is the unity of awareness and emptiness. Finally, the mind's lucidity is also empty, so there is the unity of lucidity and emptiness. These four unities are the meaning of the unborn nature: appearance-emptiness, bliss-emptiness, awareness-emptiness, and lucidity-emptiness. The instruction here is to rest in just this: "Abide continually within the mind itself and practice only deep meditation." We do this without thought, without mental activity, which means that we rest free of any dualistic differentiation between that which is meditating or observing and that which is meditated upon.

When we realize the unborn nature (emptiness), then the cause of suffering (the disturbing emotions) and its result (suffering) cease. As a result, we are liberated from misery, fear, sadness, regret, and anxiety. These are all eradicated, leaving us fearless. For this reason, the samādhi realizing the unborn was called the heroic samādhi, because achieving it, we are no longer afraid of anything.

THE FOURTH SYMBOL: BEYOND THE INTELLECT

33. Intellect, mind, and mental appearances have this very nature.
    All the worlds appearing in their diversity have this very nature.

> All the varieties of the seen and the seer have this very nature.
> Attachment, desire, aversion, and bodhicitta, too, have this very
> nature.

At the level of the fourth symbol, one realizes that the nature of the
mind is not only beyond existence but also beyond nonexistence—it is
completely beyond the intellect. Since this is attained through direct
experience, it transcends any conceptual apprehension of existence or
nonexistence and is the direct experience of the true nature just as it is,
beyond any kind of extreme. It is, therefore, the ultimate samādhi.

This fourth symbol transcends even the realization of the unborn
described in the previous verse. It is the vajralike samādhi, or the ulti-
mate samādhi. One passes through various states: (1) thoughts arising in
the mind are apprehended by mindfulness; (2) mindfulness is dissolved
into the expanse beyond mindfulness; (3) within that expanse occurs
the realization of the unborn; (4) and finally even that is transcended, so
that "Intellect, mind, and mental appearances have this very nature."
This is what is meant when it is said that this nature, or dharmatā, is
beyond the intellect, beyond mind, and beyond all mental appearances
while remaining the nature of them all. The third line, "All the varieties
of the seen and the seer have this very nature," means that though this
nature is beyond the dualism of seer and seen, all phenomena have this
nature. This is how to understand the nature that is beyond the intellect.

The fourth line of this verse states that bodhicitta also has this very
nature. In general, bodhicitta has two aspects: relative and absolute. Rel-
ative bodhicitta is the wish to protect and alleviate the suffering of all
beings. In essence, it is compassion that has an aspect of wisdom. This
verse is speaking of absolute bodhicitta, which recognizes the true nature
of all things. It also has an aspect of compassion, because the realization
of the nature of all phenomena spontaneously produces an extraordinary
compassion for all beings. This compassion is extremely powerful

because it is unfabricated. This completes an explanation of the fourth symbol, beyond the intellect.

The next question about the path that needs to be answered is, How do we start to practice these four symbols? We start through the gradual cultivation of the wisdom of listening, contemplation, and meditation. Why do we need listening? Although we all possess sugatagarbha, or buddha nature, we are unaware of it. Since we do not know it is there, we have to be told that all sentient beings including ourselves have buddha nature. An analogy for this is presented in the *Uttaratantra* where it explains that our buddha nature, which is basically a synonym for the sugatagarbha, is like buried gold. Imagine that a large piece of gold was buried underground, covered with dirt and refuse of all kinds. The gold itself would not change at all, even though a hundred or a thousand years passed. Nevertheless, no one would take advantage of it because it was hidden. Eventually, a poor person comes along and builds his shack directly over the gold. The gold could alleviate his poverty, but since he does not know it is there in the first place, he makes no use of the gold and suffers. A person with extrasensory perception comes along, observes the situation, and kindly and compassionately tells the poor person, "You know, there is a very large piece of gold directly under your shack. Why don't you remove it and take care of all your needs?" The poor man hearing this does so and is freed from the suffering of poverty. The function of listening is very much like that. You come to know the gold of buddha nature within.

Listening, Contemplation, and Meditation

34. A lamp is lit in the darkness of ignorance.
    While you differentiate mental categories,
    You discard the mind's flaws.
    Reflect upon the nature of nonattachment.

Saraha advises that when we begin to practice the path of the four symbols, we should do so gradually through generating the wisdom of listening, contemplating, and meditating. He gives this advice because we are ordinary beings at the very beginning of the path and do not understand the nature of our mind. In order to be able to entertain this idea and eventually realize it, we must initially encounter either the Buddha's teachings or the commentaries on these teachings, which are found in many texts and in the practical instructions of the mahāsiddhas, such as this song of Saraha. Of course, we have the nature of our mind within us, but we do not have access to this nature, because we follow our own confused projections and bewildered appearances. We are immersed in these incorrect thoughts and cannot reverse the bewilderment by ourselves, since it is our own bewilderment.

The first line of the verse states: "A lamp is lit in the darkness of ignorance." In this analogy, the lamp is the fact that the gold is there, that buddha nature exists. This is the beginning of the process of removing ignorance. Understanding what we have heard is the achievement of the wisdom of hearing, and it starts with encountering the Buddha's teachings.

Nevertheless, this initial hearing and the wisdom generated through it are not enough. We need to scrutinize and evaluate what has been heard. This is the wisdom of contemplation, which generates conceptual certainty. The verse states: "While you differentiate mental categories,... " which refers to a conceptual state of the mind and this cannot in itself remove defects or bewilderment, nor can it generate true wisdom. Therefore, after the wisdom of contemplation, we need to go further and cultivate the wisdom that arises from meditation. Through this, the song states that you will "discard the mind's flaws." It is this process of listening, contemplation, and meditation that allows you to realize the meaning of the four symbols.

An Extensive Explanation of Key Instructions
NOTHING TO NEGATE OR CONSTRUCT

35. There is no negating, no constructing,
    And no apprehending: it is inconceivable.
    The ignorant are bound by mental categories.
    The inseparable, the coemergent, is utterly pure.

The previous verse was an explanation of the entire process of hearing, reflection, and meditation in brief. Since the most important of these three is the practice of meditation, the next two verses continue to explain it in more detail.

Verse 35 explains that all we need to do is recognize the mind's nature; there is no need to eliminate anything from it, nor is there any need to construct some kind of logical reasoning to realize mind's nature. This same idea is explained in the *Uttaratantra:* "There is nothing to be removed from this and there is nothing to be added." "There is nothing to be removed" means that when we look at our mind's nature, we are not attempting to eliminate something from it. There is nothing solid or negative that needs to be taken out, or, as the verse says, "There is no negating."

Second, when meditating, we are not attempting to add to or improve the mind's nature: there is "no constructing." Since the nature itself is beyond the intellect and therefore cannot be conceptually understood, or apprehended, this nature is inconceivable. Those who seek for something to be negated, something to be constructed, something to be apprehended, or something to be conceptualized are referred to as "the ignorant" because they are bound by these mental categories.

Since the nature of the mind is emptiness, there is nothing that needs to be removed from it. And since the nature of the mind is not just emptiness, since it is at the same time an inherently present lucidity, there is nothing that needs to be added to it either. The quotation from the *Uttaratantra* continues: "Look perfectly at that which is perfect. If it is perfectly seen, you will be perfectly liberated." To look perfectly means to see this nature as it is, by looking at it in the right way, free of any attempt to get rid of anything or introduce anything, and also free of any conceptual stance created by a philosophical outlook. This correct seeing will bring about liberation.

What we discover in meditation is not something we can conceive of. It is utterly pure in transcending all such conceptualizations. In sum, meditation should be free of all intellectualization.

MIND IS CLEAR AND UNMOVING

36. Examining emptiness with the reasoning of one or many, you see
        that it is neither.
     Through mere recognition, living beings are utterly freed.
     Meditate recognizing what is clear and unmoving.
     I apprehend the stable mind to be just that.

Having recognized the true nature, which is emptiness, we cultivate this in meditation, which consists of fostering the continuity of the initial recognition. This is described in the third line of the verse: "Meditate recognizing what is clear and unmoving." The nature of mind that we are meditating on is totally free of any obscurations or instabilities. Even so, we can still suffer from the defects of meditation—torpor and excitement—so this line can also be understood to mean that we should meditate on emptiness with a mind that is free of both. The instruction to "meditate recognizing what is clear..." indicates that we should meditate with a mind that is not dull or lax. When the mind is unclear in this way, we need to develop the mind's lucidity, its natural clarity. The instruction to recognize what is "unmoving" means to meditate with a mind that is free of excitement or instability. When the mind is clear but agitated, we need to calm down and reduce the movement of the mind. Saraha states that by meditating on the nature of mind in this way, "I apprehend the stable mind to be just that." Through meditating with a mind that is free of the defects of torpor and excitement, we also will apprehend the nature just as it is, free of all defects and therefore clear and unmoving.

Questions

Question: Rinpoche, you stated that practicing the path of method and the path of liberation together is the most effective means of practicing. I am wondering what you meant by the path of method and why the combination is the most effective?

Rinpoche: In general, it is fine to practice the path of liberation without the path of method. What I was referring to when I said the path of method were the methods that have been passed down in the Kagyü tradition from Tilopa and Nāropa to the present day. In the Kagyü tradition, the path of liberation is defined as mahāmudrā, and the path of method refers to the six yogas of Nāropa. However, in this context the six yogas of Nāropa would also include doing yidam practices, which must precede them.

Marpa the Translator went to India three times. He said of what he brought back, "I received Hevajra, the profound tantra, and Cakrasaṃvara, the quintessence." By referring to Cakrasaṃvara as the quintessence, it is evident he considered it to be the most profound of these cycles of practice. Therefore, since the time of Marpa, the Kagyü lineage has taken that cycle as the basis for practicing the path of method. In fact, the path of method has two aspects. When method is emphasized, Cakrasaṃvara

is engaged in as the father practice. When wisdom is emphasized, Vajrayo-
ginī or Vajravārāhī is engaged in as the mother practice. Historically, we
have tended to emphasize the lineage of Vajrayoginī, whose practice has
two aspects: the generation stage of the Vajrayoginī sadhana and the com-
pletion stage of the six yogas of Nāropa. You can also understand the six
yogas of Nāropa as the completion stage of both Vajrayoginī and
Cakrasaṃvara. In the Kagyü lineage the corresponding path of libera-
tion would be the practices of tranquility and insight in the context of
mahāmudrā.

Question: Rinpoche, it was said that once you reach the first bodhisattva
level, there is no falling back. It is also said that you reach the first bodhi-
sattva level when you have had experience of mahāmudrā. My own expe-
rience has been that the path is very gradual, sometimes you click in
and sometimes you click out. Sometimes you click out for a long time
and then come back in again.

Rinpoche: There is a difference between proceeding through the path to
enlightenment by means of the profound path of the Vajrayāna, or secret
mantra, and the vast path of a bodhisattva. For example, we can com-
pare two individuals, both of whom achieved perfect awakening, the
Buddha and Milarepa. Śākyamuni Buddha gathered the accumulations
for three innumerable eons and achieved buddhahood. Milarepa
achieved the state of Vajradhara in one lifetime and one body. What
they achieved in terms of their wisdom mind and what they realized are
not different: whatever the Buddha saw, Milarepa saw. Whatever the
Buddha abandoned, Milarepa abandoned. However, their paths were
different in the way that their fruition manifested. Because the Buddha
achieved full awakening through the innumerable eons of practice, when
he achieved it, his body was adorned with the thirty-two marks and
eighty signs of physical perfection; his speech was embellished with the
sixty limbs of melody; and his activity was both perfect and pervasive.

Milarepa realized the same thing that the Buddha realized, but because of the difference in the merit accumulated, Milarepa's body was not adorned with the thirty-two marks and eighty signs, did not possess the sixty branches of melody, and his activity was not identical to that of Śākyamuni Buddha. The wisdom was the same, but there was a difference in the manifestation of the result, which is due to the difference in the manner of gathering the accumulations or, you could say, in the length and stability of the paths.

When you see the nature of your mind, you are realizing dharmatā. A first-level bodhisattva realizes dharmatā and achieves a state that will not revert to a lower level. Although we realize the same nature that is realized by a first-level bodhisattva on the vast path of the Mahayana, the circumstances, means, or conditions for our realization are different. Because we achieved this insight through what is called abrupt introduction, we do not achieve the state of irreversibility the way a bodhisattva would by realizing dharmatā. In sum, the nature that is seen by a mahāmudrā practitioner is the same as the nature seen by a first-level bodhisattva on the path of the Mahayana, but the qualities that come with those insights are different.

Fruition Mahāmudrā   5

━━━━━━━━━━━━━━━━━━━━━━━━━━━━━━━━━━━━━━━

A *Song for the King* has three main sections, presenting the ground, the path, and the fruition. We have come to the third, the fruition of mahāmudrā, which in turn has three sections. I will go through these three sections briefly, and there is a reason for doing so. The first section of the ground must be clearly explained. When we are attempting to ascertain the nature of the ground, it is essential that it be properly understood, because it is the basis of the path. In the same way, to achieve the result, the path must be properly understood so that we can correctly proceed along it and avoid mistakes. The fruition is something that we either attain or do not attain as a result of the path. It is somewhat simpler to talk about, as it requires less explanation.

Primordial Wisdom Expands through Bliss

37. Through attaining the vast land of happiness,
     And through seeing its own nature, mind becomes vast.
     You walk through the land, yet mind's nature is not separate.

The first of the three topics within the presentation of the fruition is how primordial wisdom expands when we attain great bliss. As we have seen, if we realize the nature of our mind, we are liberated from samsara. This constitutes the perfect accomplishment of benefit for oneself, and it also creates the causal condition for the complete accomplishment of benefit for others. Due to these two benefits, we experience consummate joy, and this joy is also the expansion of wisdom.

In general, the qualities of a buddha are defined as wisdom, love, and ability. Wisdom is twofold: a buddha possesses the wisdom that knows the nature of phenomena and the wisdom that knows the variety of phenomena. The wisdom that knows the true nature of phenomena is the fact that the buddha directly sees dharmatā. At the same time, a buddha also sees the individual joys and sufferings of each living being, and this is the wisdom of the variety of phenomena.

Buddhas are not only wise. Through their possession of perfect wisdom, they also have perfect loving-kindness for all beings. If the buddhas possessed only the two wisdoms and had no ability to benefit others, the situation would be quite different. But since they possess both consummate wisdom and perfect loving-kindness, they also possess the perfect ability to benefit and protect others. This explanation of the three qualities of buddhahood fills out the basic definition of fruition mahāmudrā.

All of the sufferings of samsara are due to confused projections or confused appearances. When we recognize that these are empty, we eradicate both the cause and the result of suffering, and this leads to an experience of great bliss. The song states, "Through attaining the vast land of happiness," which refers to an all-pervasive state of great bliss. Through attaining this and "through seeing its own nature, mind becomes vast." This experience of a boundless state of great bliss— although it is in one sense a ground or object of experience—is not separate from the mind that experiences it; therefore, the mind itself is vast. From a relative point of view, we experience this state of great of bliss as though it were an environment or a land we are walking through. In actuality, however, since this environment or state of great bliss has always been the nature of our mind and the nature of all things, we are inseparable from it. Therefore, the verse concludes, "Yet mind's nature is not separate."

Delineating the Five Kāyas

38. Coemergent joy is the dharmakāya. The sambhogakāya is
        the seedling of joy
    And superior; the leaves come forth.
    At the time of the path, the dharmakāya does not radiate in
        the ten directions.
    Bliss free of constructs is fruition itself.

The second topic within fruition is delineating the five kāyas through the dharmakāya's emanation of two form kāyas. This leads to an expanded layout of the dharmakāya, which accounts for the spontaneous presence of the five kāyas. The verse begins, "Coemergent joy is the dharmakāya." The ultimate result has a variety of qualities, and the distinctions among these qualities are the divisions of the various bodies. The primary and usual division of the kāyas is into the dharmakāya, the sambhogakāya, and the nirmāṇakāya. Of these three, the dharmakāya is the perfect accomplishment of benefit for oneself, while the sambhogakāya and nirmāṇakāya are the perfect accomplishment of benefit for others. In his song, Saraha speaks of five different kāyas, of which the initial three represent aspects or qualities of the dharmakāya: innate wisdom, natural purity, and great bliss.

First, it is important to understand the quality of being innate. The dharmakāya is not newly acquired at the time of fruition, nor is it something created by the path. It is the nature of mind from the very beginning. Further, its wisdom transcends the intellect, which operates in a dualistic mode of perception. The second quality is the natural purity of the dharmakāya, which is given the name *svābhāvikakāya*. From beginningless time, it is essentially pure and has never been stained. The third quality reflects the fact that the dharmakāya is not a state of nothingness nor is it suffering; it is a state of great bliss, and therefore it is also called the body of great bliss, or *mahāsukhakāya*. In this way, we can divide the dharmakāya into its qualities of innate wisdom, natural purity, and great bliss, and say there are three kāyas, but actually, these three bodies are all qualities or aspects of the dharmakāya.

While the dharmakāya of the Buddha realizes dharmatā, he displays the two form bodies in order to communicate with others. To benefit those with pure perception (the bodhisattvas), the dharmakāya displays the sambhogakāya. To help ordinary beings, it displays the supreme nirmāṇakāya, such as Śākyamuni Buddha.

To summarize, when we attain coemergent wisdom and the dharmakāya, it does not mean that the dharmakāya is created by our achievement of coemergent wisdom. It has always been purely present and is simply recognized. Since the dharmakāya is innate and not newly created, it is also called the svābhāvikakāya, or essence body, which is the second body. The state of dharmakāya is the state of coemergent joy, and since it is free of all suffering whatsoever, it is also the mahāsukhakāya, or the body of great bliss. Now these three—the dharmakāya, svābhāvika-kāya, and mahāsukhakāya—can be considered three bodies or they can be considered one, the dharmakāya.

The next two kāyas, the fourth and fifth, are the form kāyas: the *sambhogakāya* and the *nirmāṇakāya*. The sambhogakāya is "the seedling of joy," where "joy" refers to the state of great bliss, a quality of the dharmakāya. The "seedling" emerging from it is the sambhogakāya, which is "superior" to the nirmāṇakāya. Why is this so? The sambhogakāya appears only to individuals with pure faculties (bodhisattvas), while the nirmāṇakāya appears to those who have ordinary faculties and are not so pure. The sambhogakāya is the initial emanation of the dharmakāya, as a seedling first appears, and then the nirmāṇakāya emanates as the leaves growing from a stalk. This is the brief explanation of the five bodies, which can be summarized into three.

Benefit for Self and Others Is Nondual

39. Those staying in that land benefit those living there but are not
    truly existent.
    Nevertheless, there is a need that they stay in that place, benefiting those beings.
    Attached and ultimately not attached are the form kāyas;
    Emptiness is inseparable from appearance.

The third section details the fruition of mahāmudrā and explains how on the level of ultimate truth, the two form bodies, or *rūpakāyas,* do not exist. Ultimately, buddhas and sentient beings have the same nature, and so living beings have been buddhas from the very beginning. Furthermore, although buddhas abide as the dharmakāya and display the form bodies, these kāyas are not distinct from one another. There are no rūpakayās aside from the dharmakāya, and there is no dharmakāya aside from the rūpakayās. In this way, the nature of any form that is displayed is emptiness, which is the very source of that display.

The first line states: "Those staying in that land benefit those living there but are not truly existent." In ultimate truth, the two form bodies that benefit beings have no true or absolute existence. Further, those who are benefited by these two form bodies do not have true or ultimate existence either. Yet, as the second line states: "Nevertheless, there is a need that they stay in that place, benefiting those beings." This is true because within the land of relative truth, the presence of the two form bodies brings real benefit for living beings. The third line states: "Attached and ultimately not attached are the form kāyas." "Attached" here means exhibiting affection for sentient beings and refers to the two form kāyas. "Nonattached" refers to the dharmakāya, which is in itself a state of complete peace. While the two form kāyas appear to have different functions within relative truth, in ultimate truth they have no existence apart from the dharmakāya. Therefore, the fourth line states: "Emptiness is inseparable from appearance."

The Conclusion: What Is Flawless

40. It is not like a pig attached to the mire of samsara.
    Once you have realized the flawless mind, what fault is there?
    Anyone who practices like this is not affected by anything.
    Why would this person be bound by flaws?

The final verse completes the presentation of mahāmudrā's result with an explanation of how the dharmakāya, the fruition of mahāmudrā, is stainless and irreversible. The two form kāyas have come to realize this flawless nature of mind. Since they are the display of the dharmakāya, and since the dharmakāya is the realization of this stainless nature, even though they remain active in samsara, the two form bodies are not attached to cyclic existence nor stained by it. Furthermore, the verse says: "Anyone who practices like this is not affected by anything." Since this state of fruition is irreversible, when we recognize the stainless nature and attain the dharmakāya, that realization renders us impervious to any conditions. Therefore, the rhetorical question is asked, "Why would this person be bound by flaws?" Why would you think this individual would be bound, since the potential for being fettered has been eradicated?

This verse brings to a close the explanation of Saraha's *A Song for the King*. Having made a connection with this text and its explanation, I hope that you will be able to emphasize the practice of mahāmudrā in your personal practice, both in meditation and in postmeditation. There is nothing more valuable or more important, because this is what will lead to the ultimate result of Dharma practice. While you are on the path, this practice will dispel adversity. If, for one reason or another, you cannot practice with as much diligence as you wish, remember that you are still very fortunate and have benefited a great deal from connecting with these teachings. Even if you have just heard these teachings and do not practice them, you have created a positive tendency and a familiarity with them. This is always beneficial and can never be harmful. At the very least, you have once and for all determined that samsara will sooner or later come to an end for you. Therefore, please rejoice.

Appendix 1

A Song for the King
by Saraha

With an Outline and Interpolations from

The Middle-Length Commentary on "A Song for the King":
A Mirror Revealing the Complete Liberation of Mind

By Karma Trinlépa

There are three main divisions:
I. The Introduction
II. The Main Section
III. The Conclusion

I. The Introduction
    A. The meaning of the title
    1. The translation of the title

In the Indian language, the title is *Doha Kosha Nama Tsarya Giti.*
In Tibetan, it is *Doha mdzod ces bya ba spyod pa'i glu.* [*(From) the*
Treasury of Spiritual Songs, A Song of Yogic Conduct.]

From the four families of languages in India, there is a natural language
found in the land of coconuts in the south. For this language, the title
of the doha, or spiritual song, is "Dwaha Kosha Nama Tsarya Giti,"
which was translated into Tibetan as "[From] the Treasury of Spiritual
Songs, A Song of Yogic Conduct." It is possible to link the Tibetan and

the Indian language of the translation. There are many meanings that can be applied to the word *Dwaha:* leaving aside the Tibetan here, in Sanskrit this term was given as "Doha." *Kosha* was translated into Tibetan as *mdzod* [treasury], *nama* as *zhes bya ba* [called], *tsarya* as *spyod pa* [conduct], and *giti* as *glu* [song].

2. An explanation of the title

The explanation of *A Treasury of Spiritual Songs* is similar to the one given in "A Song for the People." *Called* is a grammatical term that indicates the title, and "A Song of Yogic Conduct" comes from the fact that it is a song of one who is engaged in yogic activity or conduct, so it is [also] said to be a "vajra song."

B. The homage of the translator

I prostrate to Noble Mañjuśrī.

II. The Main Section
   A. Homage to the deity who delights
   B. A teaching on the condensed essence of the ground, path, and fruition
   C. A separate explanation of these [three]

II.A. Homage to the deity to who delights

I prostrate to the one who has vanquished the power of the māras.

II.B. A teaching on the condensed essence of the ground, path, and fruition

1. Three examples show how the ground, though utterly pure, appears as delusion.
2. The examples of water and of light or darkness show how [when we are on] the path, wisdom that realizes [emptiness] purifies ignorance.
3. The example of the ocean shows that the fruition is free of increase or decrease.

In the first section here, there are three categories:
a) The example of waves shows how delusive appearances arise within the ground.
b) The example of the double appearance of lamps, caused by delusion, shows how subject and object appear to be separate.
c) The example of the lamp and darkness shows how we do not realize that primordial wisdom pervades the outside [world].

II.B.1.a) The example of waves shows how delusive appearances arise within the ground.

> *Just as when the wind blows*
> *And still water is turned into moving waves,*
> *So the appearing Saraha is just one,*
> *Yet the king creates diverse aspects.* [verse 1]

II.B.1.b) The example of the double appearance of lamps, caused by delusion, shows how subject and object appear to be separate.

> *The ignorant press their eyes*[53]
> *And see one lamp as two.*

Like this, in [mind's nature] where seer and seen are not two,
Alas! The mind appears as two things. [verse 2]

II.B.1.c) The example of the lamp and darkness shows how we do not realize that primordial wisdom pervades the outside [world].

Though many lamps are lit throughout the house,
Those with no eyes to see remain in darkness.
Like this, though spontaneous wisdom is all-pervasive and nearby,
For the ignorant it is far, far away. [verse 3]

II.B.2. The examples of water and of light or darkness show how [when we are on] the path, wisdom that realizes [emptiness] purifies ignorance.

Though diverse, rivers are one in the ocean.
Though myriad, lies are overcome by a single truth.
Though darkness is manifold,
The rising of a single sun clears it away. [verse 4]

II.B.3. The example of the ocean shows that the fruition is free of increase or decrease.
  a) Setting forth the example
  b) Showing its meaning

II.B.3.a) Setting forth the example

Though cloud banks take up water from the ocean
And fill the earth again [with descending rains],
[The ocean] does not decrease; [filling] the whole sky, it [remains full]:
There is no increase or decrease. [verse 5]

II B.3.b) Showing its meaning

> *The Victorious Ones are filled with perfect [qualities],*
> *Which all have the very same nature—spontaneous presence.*
> *From [the natural display of the great sphere], living beings take*
>   *birth and therein cease.*
> *In relation to this, there is no thing and no nonthing.* [verse 6]

II.C.1. Explaining in detail the phenomena connected with the
    ground
  2. Explaining how to bring the path of mahāmudrā into our
    experience
  3. Revealing the fruition

This first section has four divisions:
  a) On the basis of four incongruent analogies, advice on how to
    give up attachment
  b) On the basis of four congruent analogies, identifying the mean-
    ing indicated
  c) On the basis of mingling incongruent and congruent analogies,
    showing the way of indicating the essential nature
  d) Through two incongruent analogies, showing the interdepend-
    ent arising of cause and effect

This first section also has four divisions:
  (1) Through the example of honey in the rock, giving up attach-
    ment to conditioned bliss

Giving up genuine bliss, you take another [path]
And place your hopes in conditioned bliss.
Taking nectar in their mouth, [bees] come close,
But not drinking, they are far from [enjoyment]. [verse 7]

(2) Through the example of an ignorant expert, discarding attachment to what is to be taken and given up

Having gone astray, the [animals] do not create suffering;
On the basis of [this human life], experts create suffering.
On one hand, [practitioners] come to drink the nectar of space;
On the other, [experts] remain very attached to objects. [verse 8]

(3) Through the example of bugs in the midst of excrement, giving up attachment to contaminated bliss

Bugs on excrement are attached to its smell
And think the pure fragrance of sandalwood foul.
Likewise, attached to dense [ignorance], the source of samsara,
[Individuals] toss away the transcendence of suffering. [verse 9]

(4) Through the example of water in a hoofprint, giving up attachment to signs and indications

[The ignorant think] an ox's hoofprint filled with water [is the
   ocean and look for gems therein],
Yet [soon] this water will evaporate. Likewise, [those who take
   their passing experiences to be enlightenment]
Will not [see] the perfect [qualities]. [By developing] a stable and
   perfect mind,
[The mind clinging to passing experience as] perfect will evaporate.
   [verse 10]

II.C.1.b) On the basis of four congruent analogies, identifying the meaning indicated

This section has four divisions:

(1) Through the example of something salty becoming sweet, showing that once we have realization, there is no fault no matter how one behaves

Just as the ocean's salty water
Taken into the clouds turns sweet,
The stable mind works to benefit others;
The poison [of] objects turns into healing nectar. [verse 11]

(2) Through the example of thunder and so forth, showing that once we have realized what cannot be expressed, though fear arises at the mere mention of emptiness, it will mature into great bliss

When [you realize] the ineffable, it is neither suffering [nor bliss].
When there is nothing to meditate upon, [wisdom] itself is bliss.
Likewise, though thunder may evoke fear,
The falling of rain makes harvests ripen. [verse 12]

(3) Through the example of making no differentiation among the three times, showing that appearances and emptiness are not dual

First [a thing] and in the end [a nonthing—neither is established];
  likewise, there is nothing other than [these two].
There is no [place] to abide in the beginning, middle, or end.
For those whose minds are obscured by continual concepts,
Emptiness and compassion are expressed in words. [verse 13]

(4) Through the example of the bee and the frog, showing the difference between an expert and an ignorant person when it comes to the meaning of samsara and nirvana being inseparable

Just as the nectar dwelling within a flower
Is known by the bumblebee,
[The fortunate] toss away neither existence nor nirvana.
Like them, the ignorant should fully understand. [verse 14]

II.C.1.c) On the basis of mingling incongruent and congruent analogies, showing the way of indicating the essential nature

This section has four divisions:
(1) Through the example of a mirror's reflection, illustrating nonattachment to what is not true

Just as an image appears on the mirror's surface,
[Where] the ignorant look in their lack of knowledge,
So the mind that throws away the truth
Relies on many [concepts] that are not true. [verse 15]

(2) Through the example of a fragrant flower, showing that meditative concentration is continuous when we have realized the wheel of the three kāyas

Though the fragrance of a flower has no form,
It clearly pervades everywhere.
Likewise, through the formless nature
The circles of the mandalas will be known. [verse 16]

(3) Through the example of ice, showing how concepts are con-
cretized into something hard and dense when habitual patterns
of clinging increase

When a [wintry] wind strikes and stirs up water,
Though soft, [it] takes the form of stone.
When concepts [attempt to] disturb [mind's nature], where igno-
*   rance cannot take form,*
Appearances become very dense and solid. [verse 17]

(4) Through the example of a jewel and a swamp, showing that
mind itself is not affected by stains

The true nature of any state of mind is free of flaws
And unaffected by the mire of existence and nirvana.
Even so, if a supreme gem is placed in a swamp,
Its radiance will not be clear. [verse 18]

II.C.1.d) Through two incongruent analogies, showing the dependent
arising of cause and effect

This section has two divisions:
(1) Through the example of a seedling, showing how the ālaya (all-
basis) matures into both samsara and nirvana

When stupidity is clear, wisdom is unclear.
When stupidity is clear, suffering is clear.
Like this, from a seed, a seedling arises;
With this seedling as a cause, offshoots appear. [verse 19]

(2) Through the example of self-destruction, showing how experts are seen to lapse into the ordinary through their attachment to examining and analyzing

In analyzing the mind [with the reasoning of being] neither one nor many,
[If] you discard the clear [aspect of mind's nature], you will descend to the [lower] realms;
While gazing at [that suffering], you fall into its bottomless pit.
How could one have anything but compassion for this? [verse 20]

II.C.2. Explaining how to bring the path of mahāmudrā into our experience
a)   Discarding attachment to mistaken paths
b)   The actual path of mahāmudrā

The first section has eight divisions:
(1) Through the story of Kamarūpa, making clear the fault of attachment to a karmamudrā

Once totally attached to kissing [and] the bliss [of what follows],
The ignorant say that this is indeed the ultimate.
Having left his house, he stands in front of the gate,
Soliciting tales of sensual pleasure. [verse 21]

(2) Through the example of a royal one, making clear the fault of being attached to our body as endowed with skillful means

For the sake of the winds, [you meditate] on [your body as] an empty house,

Practicing artificial [means] in great variety and number.
From space it falls along with faults.
Overwhelmed, the yogi faints away. [verse 22]

(3) Through the example of the Brahmin's burnt offerings, making clear the fault of being bound by passing experiences

Just as Brahmins make their burnt offerings
Of ghee and rice in a blazing fire,
Know that, from [Haṃ], the quintessence of space, the substance
    [of nectar] produces experience;
The [passing experience of bliss] is grasped as reality. [verse 23]

(4) Through the example of another's mind stream, making clear the fault of contrived practice

Some make the firelight burn and [bring it to] their fontanel;
With their tongue they enjoy union with the smaller one.
This binds them up and makes them thoroughly disturbed.
Swayed by pride, they call themselves yogis. [verse 24]

(5) Through the example of a trinket and a emerald, making clear the fault of revealing to others our experience and realization

[An experience of] self-awareness, [a mere name], they display
    with [a proud] intellect.
"Whatever binds, that itself liberates," so they say.
Not knowing how to appraise a gem, the ignorant
Single out the color [green] to say that some trinket is an emerald.
    [verse 25]

(6) Through the example of confusing brass with gold, making
clear the fault of clinging to passing experiences as realization

This is bringing brass to mind as gold.
[You think] carrying this experience [onto the path] will accom-
plish the ultimate.
[That is like] being attached to the bliss of a dream.
You claim that aggregates are impermanent and bliss is permanent?
[verse 26]

(7) Through the example of a reflection, making clear the mistake
of confusing the meaning and the example *E Vam* with the
four seals

The letters E Vam *make themselves understood.*
By classifying [four] moments, the four seals are set out.
Some claim that through experiences, spontaneous presence
[appears].
[Do not be] like [the one attached] to the mirror's reflection.
[verse 27]

(8) Through the example of hallucination, making clear the fault
of establishing the ultimate based on the relative

Not understanding, the deer runs
In confusion after the water's mirage.
Likewise, the ignorant cannot [evade] thirst, and die.
Claiming it is ultimate, some take up bliss. [verse 28]

II.C.2.b) The actual path of mahāmudrā

    (1) A brief explanation based on the special pith instruction of the four symbols

> *The relative truth [refers to mindfulness]; nonminding*
> *[Points to] those mental states when the mind is released from*
>   *[mindfulness].*
> *When completely transformed, this is the supreme of the supreme.*
> *[The result] is the genuine supreme. Friends, you should know*
>   *these.* [verse 29]

    (2) Explaining each of these in detail

This has four divisions:

    (a) Having realized nonminding to be the samādhi of the lion's play, we are not affected by the swamp, given as an example.

> *The mind released from mindfulness engages in samādhi.*
> *It is completely purified of the afflictions.*
> *As the [utpala] born from a swamp is not stained by it,*
> *So [the mind itself] is not affected by the faults arising from*
>   *samsara nor by the qualities found in the Victorious One.*
>   [verse 30]

    (b) Showing that having realized mindfulness to be the samādhi that realizes everything to be like an illusion, [we know] the unmoving and the inconceivable.

[Mindfulness] also sees with certainty that all [things] are like an illusion.
Transcending the world, [take] this moment [into your mind] and rest evenly in meditation.
Those whose minds [recognize] the teaching bind up ignorance.
Self-arising and inconceivable, [wisdom] naturally abides [within]. [verse 31]

(c) Showing that having realized the unborn to be the samādhi of the hero's stride, we transcend samsara

These appearances have [the nature of] clarity; from the very first they are unborn.
They do not [arise as an entity] with form; discard [as well thinking they arise] in the aspect of form's characteristics.
Abide continually within the [mind] itself and practice only deep meditation.
Without thought, [rest] in this meditation free of mental activity and free of flaws. [verse 32]

(d) Having realized "beyond the mind" to be the vajralike samādhi, showing to the practitioner—through all phenomena not being separate—the very nature of mahāmudrā

Intellect, mind, and mental appearances have this very nature.
All the worlds appearing in their diversity have this very nature.
All the varieties of the seen and the seer have this very nature.
Attachment, desire, aversion, and bodhicitta, too, have this very nature. [verse 33]

(3) Explaining in general how to practice with the lamp that is the mindfulness of the ālaya (the all-basis) through listening, reflection, and meditation

A lamp is lit in the darkness of ignorance.
While you differentiate mental categories,
You discard the mind's flaws.
Reflect upon the nature of nonattachment. [verse 34]

(4) An extensive explanation of key instructions on meditation, such as teaching that with realization, there is no negating and no constructing

(a) A presentation [showing] that once [mind's nature] is realized, there is nothing to negate or construct; it is not vitiated by the flaws of tenets and systems

There is no negating, no constructing,
And no apprehending: it is inconceivable.
The ignorant are bound by mental categories.
The inseparable, the coemergent, is utterly pure. [verse 35]

(b) A presentation showing how, through comprehending and attaining great bliss, the mind is liberated, clear, and unmoving; there is nothing to be meditated upon

Examining [emptiness] with [the reasoning of] one or many, [you
see that] it is neither.
Through mere recognition, living beings are utterly freed.
Meditate recognizing what is clear and unmoving.
I apprehend the stable mind to be [just] that. [verse 36]

II.C.3. Explaining the flawless result

a) Through the attainment of great bliss, primordial wisdom expands.

> *Through attaining the vast land of happiness,*
> *And through seeing [its own nature], mind becomes vast.*
> *You walk through the land, yet [mind's nature] is not separate.*
> [verse 37][54]

b) Delineating the five kāyas through the emanation of two form kāyas from the dharmakāya, which is free of mental constructs

> *[Coemergent] joy [is the dharmakāya]. [The sambhogakāya] is the*
>   *seedling of joy*
> *And superior; the leaves come forth.*
> *At the time [of the path, the dharmakāya] does not radiate in the*
>   *ten directions.*
> *Bliss free of constructs is fruition itself.* [verse 38]

c) Since, ultimately, sentient beings and the buddhas are not established at all, the benefit for ourselves and for others is nondual.

> *Those [staying] in that [land benefit] those [living] there [but] are*
>   *not [truly] existent.*
> *[Nevertheless,] there is a need that they [stay] in that [place,*
>   *benefiting] those [beings].*
> *Attached and [ultimately] not attached are the form [kāyas];*
> *Emptiness is [inseparable from appearance].* [verse 39]

III. The Conclusion (by way of showing the meaning of what is
flawless)

> *[It is not like a] pig attached to the mire of samsara.*
> *[Once] you have realized the flawless mind, what fault is there?*
> *Any[-one who practices] like this is not affected by anything.*
> *Why would [this person] be bound by flaws?* [verse 40]

These verses were composed directly by glorious Saraha, great lord of
practitioners. This concludes *A Song of Yogic Conduct* from *The Treasury
of Spiritual Songs*. It was translated from the Indian original into Tibetan
by the bilingual Nepali, Lama Asu.

Appendix 2

A Song for the King in Tibetan

༄༅། །རྒྱ་གར་སྐད་དུ། དོ་ཧ་ཀོ་ཥ་མ་ཚ་རྒྱི་ཏེ། བོད་སྐད་དུ།
དོ་ཧ་མཛོད་ཅེས་བྱ་བ་སྟོད་པའི་སྒྲ།

འཕགས་པ་འཇམ་དཔལ་ལ་ཕྱག་འཚལ་ལོ།།

བདུད་ཀྱི་སྟོབས་རབ་ཏུ་འཇོམས་པ་ལ་ཕྱག་འཚལ་ལོ།།

1. རྗེ་ལྷར་རྨོང་གིས་བརྒྱབ་པས་མི་གཡོ་བའི།།

རྒྱ་ལ་གཡོ་བས་ཏ་རྣབས་རྣམས་སུ་འགྱུར།།

དེ་ལྟར་རྒྱལ་པོས་མདའ་བསྐུན་སྟོང་བ་ཡང་།།

གཅིག་ཏིད་ན་ཡང་རྣམ་པ་སྣ་ཚོགས་བྱེད།།

2. རྗེ་ལྟར་རྟོངས་པས་བརྟོག་ནས་བསྒྲས་པ་ཡིས།།

མར་མེ་གཅིག་ཏིད་གཉིས་སུ་སྟོང་བ་ལྟར།།

དེ་ལ་བསླུ་བྱ་ལྟ་བྱེད་གཉིས་མེད་ལ།།

ཀྱི་མ་བློ་ནེ་གཉིས་ཀྱི་དངོས་པོར་སྟོང་།།

3. ཁྲིམ་དུ་ཨར་མེ་མནད་པོ་སྤྱུར་གྱུར་ཀྱང་།།

མིག་མེད་པ་ལ་མུན་པར་གནས་པ་ལྟར།།

སྤྲན་ཚིག་སྐྱེས་པས་ཐམས་ཅད་ཁྲུབ་བྱུས་ཀྱང་།།

ཉེ་ཡང་རྟོངས་པ་དགའ་ལ་ཞིན་དུ་རིང་།།

4. ཆུ་བོ་སྤུ་ཚོགས་པ་ཡང་རྒྱ་མཚོ་གཅིག་ཉིད་དང་།།

བརྟུན་པ་དུ་མ་དགའ་ཀྱང་བདེན་པ་གཅིག་གིས་འཇོམས།།

ཉེ་མ་གཅིག་དང་སྤུང་བར་གྱུར་པ་ཡིས།།

མུན་པ་དུ་མ་དགའ་ཀྱང་འཇོམས་པར་བྱེད།།

5. ཇི་ལྟར་རྒྱ་འཛིན་གྱིས་ནི་རྒྱ་མཚོ་ལས།།

ཆུ་བླངས་ནས་ནི་ས་གཞི་གང་བྱས་ཀྱང་།།

དེ་ནི་མ་ཉམས་ནམ་མཁའ་དག་དང་མཉམ།།

འཐེལ་བ་མེད་ཅིང་འགྱིབ་པ་དགའ་ཀྱང་མེད།།

6. རྒྱལ་བའི་ཕུན་སུམ་ཚོགས་པས་ཡོངས་གང་བའི།།

སྤྲན་ཚིག་སྐྱེས་པ་གཅིག་གི་རང་བཞིན་ཉིད།།

དེ་ལས་འགྱོ་བ་སྐྱེ་ཞིང་འཕགས་པ་སྟེ།།

དེ་ལ་དངོས་དང་དངོས་པོ་མེད་པའང་མེད།།

7.   དམ་པའི་བདེ་བ་སྟོངས་ནས་གཞན་དུ་འགྲོ།
       རྒྱུན་ལས་སྐྱེས་པའི་བདེ་ལ་རེ་བར་བྱེད།།
       རང་གི་ཁར་བཅུག་སྟོང་རྟེ་ཉེ་བ་ནི།།
       འཐུང་བར་མི་བྱེད་ཤིན་ཏུ་རིང་བར་འགྱུར།།

8.   བྲོལ་སོང་དགའ་གིས་སྲུག་བསྲལ་མི་བྱེད་ལ།།
       མཁས་པ་དགའ་གིས་དེ་ལ་སྲུག་བསྲལ་བྱེད།།
       ཅིག་ཤོས་ནས་མཁའི་བདུད་རྟེ་འཐུང་བར་བྱེད།།
       གཞན་ནི་ཡུལ་རྣམས་དགའ་ལའང་རྣམ་པར་ཆག

9.   བཕང་བའི་སྲིན་བུ་དྲི་ལ་ཆགས་པ་ནི།།
       ཚ་ཚུན་དགའ་ལ་དྲི་དན་དགའ་ཏུ་སེམས།།
       དེ་ལྟར་སྐྱུ་དན་འདས་པ་སྟོངས་ནས་ནི།།
       སྲིད་པའི་འབྱུང་གནས་མཐུག་པས་ཆགས་པར་བྱེད།།

10.   བ་སྐྱོང་ཀྱང་རྗེས་རྒྱ་ཡིས་གང་བྱས་ཀྱང་།།
       རྗེ་ལྟར་དེ་ཡང་སྐྱམ་པར་འགྱུར་བ་བཞིན།།
       ཕུན་ཚོགས་མ་ཡིན་ཕུན་ཚོགས་བཟུན་པའི་སེམས།།
       ཡང་ན་ཕུན་སུམ་ཚོགས་པ་སྐྱམ་པར་འགྱུར།།

11.   ཇི་ལྟར་རྒྱུ་མཚོ་བ་ཆུ་ཅན་གྱི་ཆུ།།

རྒྱུ་འཛིན་ཁ་ཡིས་བླངས་པས་མངར་བར་འགྱུར།།

བཏན་པའི་སེམས་ཀྱིས་གཞན་གྱི་དོན་བྱེད་དང་།།

ཡུལ་གྱི་དུག་ཀྱང་བདུད་རྩིར་འགྱུར་བ་ཡིན།།

12.   བརྗོད་དུ་མེད་ན་སྨྲག་བསྒྱལ་མ་ཡིན་ཏེ།།

བསྒོམ་དུ་མེད་ན་དེ་ཉིད་བདེ་བ་ཡིན།།

ཇི་ལྟར་འབྲུག་གི་སྒྲ་ཡིས་དངངས་ན་ཡང་།།

ཆར་པ་བབ་པས་ལོ་ཏོག་སྨྱིན་པར་བྱེད།།

13.   དང་པོ་ཐ་མ་དེ་བཞིན་གཞན་ན་མེད།།

ཐོག་མ་ཐ་མ་བར་དུ་གནས་པ་མེད།།

ཀུན་ཏུ་ཏོག་པས་རྟོངས་པའི་ཡིད་ཅན་ལ།།

སྟོང་པ་དང་ནི་སྟོང་རྗེ་བརྗོད་པས་སོ།།

14.   ཇི་ལྟར་མེ་ཏོག་ནང་གནས་སྦྲང་རྩི་ནི།།

བུང་བ་ཉིད་ཀྱིས་ཤེས་པར་འགྱུར་བ་ཡིན།།

སྲིད་དང་རྒྱུ་ངན་འདས་པ་མི་འདོར་རོ།།

རྨོངས་པ་དག་གིས་ཇི་ལྟར་ཡོངས་སུ་ཤེས།།

15. ཇི་ལྟར་མེ་ལོང་དག་ས་སུ་བཞིན་གྱི་གཟུགས།།

 སྣང་ངས་པ་མི་ཤེས་པ་ཡིས་བལྟས་པ་ལྟར།།

དེ་ལྟར་བདེན་པ་སྒྲུངས་པའི་སེམས་འདི་ནི།།

མི་བདེན་པ་ལ་མང་དུ་བརྟེན་པར་བྱེད།།

16. མེ་ཏོག་དྲི་ནི་གཟུགས་སུ་མེད་ན་ཡང་།།

མཆོ་སུམ་ཀུན་ཏུ་ཁྱབ་པར་བྱེད་པ་ལྟར།།

དེ་བཞིན་གཟུགས་སུ་མེད་པའི་རང་བཞིན་གྱིས།།

དགྱིལ་འཁོར་འཁོར་ལོ་དག་ཀྱང་ཤེས་པར་གྱིས།།

17. སྣང་གིས་རྒྱ་ལ་ཞུགས་ཤིང་དཀྱུགས་པ་ཡིས།།

འཇམ་པའི་རྒྱ་ཡང་རྡོ་ཡི་གཟུགས་ལྟར་འགྱོ།།

ཏྟོག་པས་དཀྱུགས་པས་རྫོངས་པ་གཟུགས་མེད་པ།།

ཤིན་ཏུ་སུ་ཞིང་མཐེགས་པ་ཉིད་དུ་འགྱུར།།

18. སེམས་གང་དུ་ཨ་མེད་པའི་རང་བཞིན་ལ།།

སྱིད་དང་ལྱུང་འདས་འདམ་གྱིས་མ་གོས་སོ།།

འདམ་དུ་བཙུག་ན་མཆོག་གི་རིན་པོ་ཆེ།།

དེ་ཡི་འོད་ཀྱང་གསལ་བ་མ་ཡིན་ནོ།།

19.　　གཏི་མུག་གསལ་བས་ཡེ་ཤེས་མི་གསལ་ཏེ།།

　　　　གཏི་མུག་གསལ་བས་སྟུག་བསྐུལ་གསལ་བ་ཡིན།།

　　　　ཇི་ལྟར་ས་བོན་ལས་ནེ་མྱུ་གུ་འབྱུང་།།

　　　　མྱུ་གུའི་རྒྱུ་ལས་ཡལ་ག་འབྱུང་བཞོ།།

20.　　གཅིག་དང་དུ་མ་སེམས་ལ་དཔྱད་པ་ཡིས།།

　　　　གསལ་བ་སྒྱུངས་ནས་སྙིང་པ་དག་ཏུ་འགྲོ།

　　　　མཐོང་བཞིན་དུ་ནི་དོང་དུ་འགྲོ་བ་ལ།།

　　　　དེ་ལས་སྙིང་རྗེ་བ་ནི་ཅི་ཞིག་ཡོད།།

21.　　ཁ་སྦྱོར་བདེ་ལ་ཡོངས་སུ་ཆགས་ནས་སུ།།

　　　　འདི་ཉིད་དོན་དམ་ཡིན་ཞེས་རྟོངས་པ་སྟ།

　　　　དེ་ནི་ཁྲིམ་ནས་བྱུང་ནས་སྒོ་དྲུང་དུ།།

　　　　ཀ་མ་དུ་པའི་གཏམ་ནི་འདྲེ་བར་བྱེད།།

22.　　སྦྲང་གི་རྒྱུ་ལས་སྦྱོང་པའི་ཁྲིམ་དུ་ནི།།

　　　　རྣམ་པ་དུ་མའི་ཆུལ་གྱིས་བཅོས་མ་བྱས།།

　　　　ནམ་མཁའ་ལས་བབ་ཉེས་པ་དང་བཅས་པའི།།

　　　　གདུང་བས་བརྒྱལ་བར་གྱུར་པའི་རྣལ་འབྱོར་པ།།

23. ཇི་ལྟར་བྲམ་ཟེ་མར་དང་འབྲས་ཀྱིས་ནི།།

འབར་བའི་མེ་ལ་སྤྲིན་སྲེག་བྱེད་པ་ནི།།

ནམ་མཁའི་བཅུད་ཀྱི་རྫས་ཀྱིས་བསྐྱེད་པ་སྟེ།།

འདི་ནེ་ཉིད་དུ་ཞེན་པར་ཤེས་པ་ཉིད།།

24. ཁ་ཅིག་ཆོངས་པའི་གནས་སུ་འོད་སྦྱར་ནས།།

ལྔེ་ཡིས་ཀུན་དུ་རུ་ཡིས་ལྔེ་ཅུང་བསྐྱོད།།

འཆིང་བར་བྱེད་པ་ཤིན་ཏུ་དཀྱུགས་བྱས་ཏེ།།

ང་རྒྱལ་དབང་གིས་རྣལ་འབྱོར་པ་ཞེས་ཟེར།།

25. རང་རིག་དེ་ཉིད་རིག་པས་གཞན་ལ་སྟོན།།

གང་གིས་བཅིངས་པ་དེ་ཉིད་གྲོལ་ཞེས་ཟེར།།

ཁ་དོག་དབྱེ་བས་འཆིད་བུ་མ་རྐྱད་ཟེར།།

རྨོངས་པས་རིན་ཆེན་བཏག་པ་མ་ཤེས་པས།།

26. དེ་ནི་ར་གན་གསེར་གྱི་བློ་ཡིས་ལེན།།

ཉམས་སྤྱོད་ཁྱེར་ནས་དོན་དམ་སྒྲུབ་པར་བྱེད།།

རྨི་ལམ་བདེ་ལ་རྗེས་སུ་ཆགས་པར་བྱེད།།

ཕྱུག་པོ་མི་ཧྲག་བདེ་བ་ཧྲག་ཅེས་ཟེར།།

27.   ཨེ་སྨ་ཨེ་གོར་རང་གིས་གོ་བར་བྱེད།།

སྣད་ཚིག་དབྱེ་བས་ཕྱུག་བརྒྱ་བཞི་བཀོད་ཅིང་།།

ཉམས་སུ་སྤྱོང་བས་ལྡན་ཚིག་སྐྱེས་པ་ཟེར།།

གཟུགས་བརྐུན་ཞེན་པ་མེ་ལོང་ལྟ་བ་བཞིན།།

28.   ཇི་ལྟར་མ་རྟོགས་སྐྱིག་རྒྱུའི་ཆུ་ལ་ནི།།

འཁྱལ་པའི་དབང་གིས་རི་དགས་རྒྱུག་པར་བྱེད།།

རྫོངས་པ་སྨོ་པ་མི་ནུས་འཆི་བར་འགྱུར།།

གང་ཞིག་དོན་དམ་ཟེར་ཞིང་བདེ་བ་ལེན།།

29.   ཀུན་རྟོབ་བདེན་པ་དུན་པ་མེད་པ་སྟེ།།

སེམས་གང་སེམས་ནི་མེད་པར་གྱུར་པའོ།།

དེ་ཉིད་ཡོངས་སུ་གྱུར་པ་མཆོག་གི་མཆོག།

མཆོག་གི་དམ་པ་གྲོགས་དགའ་ཞེས་པར་གྱིས།།

30.   སེམས་ནི་དུན་མེད་ཏིང་རེ་འཛིན་དུ་སྦྱར།།

ཉོན་མོངས་ཡོངས་སུ་དག་པའང་དེ་ཉིད་དོ།།

ཇི་ལྟར་འདམ་སྐྱེས་འདམ་གྱིས་མི་གོས་བཞིན།།

སྲིད་འབྱུང་ཉེས་པས་རྒྱལ་ཚོས་མི་གོས་སོ།།

31. དེ་ཡང་ཐམས་ཅད་སྒྱུ་མར་དེས་པར་བལྟ་བུ་སྟེ།།

 འཇིག་རྟེན་འདས་པ་སྐྱད་ཅིག་ལེན་དང་བཅད་སྙོམས་བྱེད།།

བསྐྱན་པའི་བློ་ཅན་དེ་དག་གཏི་མུག་འཆིང་བར་འགྱུར།།

རང་བྱུང་བསམ་གྱིས་མི་ཁྱབ་རང་བཞིན་གནས་པ་ཡིན།།

32. སྐྱང་འདི་གསལ་བར་དང་པོ་ཉིད་ནས་མ་སྐྱེས་ཏེ།།

གཟུགས་ཅན་མ་ཡིན་གཟུགས་ཀྱི་རང་བཞིན་རྣམ་པར་སྤངས།།

དེ་ཉིད་རྒྱུན་དུ་གནས་ཤིང་བསམ་གཏན་གཅིག་བུ་བྱེད།།

ཡིད་ལ་མི་བྱེད་དེ་མེད་བསམ་གཏན་སེམས་མ་ཡིན།།

33. བློ་དང་སེམས་དང་སེམས་ཀྱི་སྐྱང་བ་དེ་བདག་ཉིད།།

འཇིག་རྟེན་གང་དག་གཞན་དུ་སྐྱང་བ་དེ་བདག་ཉིད།།

སྐུ་ཚོགས་མ་ལུས་མཐོང་བུ་མཐོང་བྱེད་དེ་བདག་ཉིད།།

ཆགས་སྐྱང་གཏི་མུག་བྱུང་རྒྱབ་སེམས་ཀྱང་དེ་བདག་ཉིད།།

34. གཏི་མུག་མུན་པར་སྒྲིན་མི་སྲུར།།

ཇི་སྲིད་བློ་ཡི་དབྱེ་བས་ཐེ།།

དེ་སྲིད་སེམས་ཀྱི་དེ་མ་སྦྱངས།།

མ་ཞིན་རང་བཞིན་གང་ཞིག་བསམ།།

35.   དགག་པ་མེད་ཅིང་སྒྲུབ་པ་མེད།།

 འཛིན་པ་མེད་དེ་བསམ་མི་ཁྱབ།།

བློ་ཡི་དབྱེ་བས་རྟོངས་རྣམས་འཆིང་།།

དབྱེར་མེད་ལྷུན་ཅིག་སྐྱེས་རྣ་དག   །

36.   གཅིག་དང་དུ་མས་རྣམ་བཏགས་གཅིག་ཉིད་མིན།།

ཤེས་པ་ཆོམ་གྱིས་འགྲོ་བ་རྣམ་པར་གྲོལ།།

གསལ་བ་གང་ཞིག་ཤེས་པ་བསྒོམ་པ་བཏན།།

མི་གཡོའི་སེམས་ནི་བདག་ཉིད་དེ་རུ་གཟུང་།།

37.   དགའ་བ་རྒྱས་པའི་ཡུལ་ཐོབ་པ།།

མཐོང་བས་སེམས་ནི་རྣམ་པར་རྒྱས།།

ཡུལ་ལ་ཕོས་ཀྱང་ཐ་དད་མེད།།

38.   དགའ་བ་བདེ་བའི་སྨྱུ་གུ་དང་།།

མཚོག་གི་འདབ་མ་སྐྱེད་པ་སྟེ།།

ཇི་སྲིད་ཕྱོགས་བཅུར་མི་འཕོ་བ།།

ཕྱོས་མེད་བདེ་བའི་འབྲས་བུ་ཉིད།།

39.   གང་གིས་གང་དུ་གང་ལ་དེ་དག་མེད།།

དེ་ཡིས་དེ་རུ་དེ་ལ་དགོས་པ་བྱས།།

རྟེས་སུ་ཆགས་པ་དང་ནི་མ་ཆགས་པའི།།

གཟུགས་ཉིད་དག་ནི་སྟོང་པ་ཉིད་ཡིན་ནོ།།

40.   སྲིད་པའི་འདམ་ཞེན་ཐག་ལྷ་བུ།།

དི་མེད་སེམས་བྱུང་སྐྱོན་ཅི་ཡོད།།

གང་ཡང་དག་གིས་མ་གོས་པ།།

དེ་ཡང་དེ་ཡིས་ཅི་ཕྱིར་འཆིང་།།

རྣལ་འབྱོར་གྱི་དབང་ཕྱུག་ཆེན་པོ་དཔལ་ས་ར་ཧའི་ཞལ་སྔ་ནས་མཛད་པ།

དོ་ཧ་མཛོད་ཅེས་བྱ་བ་སྒྱུད་པའི་གླུ་རྫོགས་སོ།།

Appendix 3

A Comparison of the Root Texts

The following annotations list the discrepancies between two recensions of the Tibetan root text and show the chosen rendering in bold. These annotations are listed in the first column by verse and line. The first recension of the text is the root text (RT) as it appears in the Dergé edition. The second version is the text as it appears in Karma Trinlépa's commentary (KTL). Many of the preferred readings were established through consulting Thrangu Rinpoche (TR).

VERSE / LINE	RT VERSION	KTL VERSION	NOTE
1b	52.6: *ba'i*	165.3: **bas**	TR prefers KTL
1d	53.1: **rnam pa**	165.6: *snang ba*	
2a	53.1: **bzlog**	166.1: *log*	
3d	53.2: *du*	166.5: **tu**	
6c	53.4: **las**	169.4: *de la*	
7c	53.5: **sbrang rtsi**	171.1: missing	
8b	53.5: **dag**	171.4: *rnams*	
8c	53.4: **cig**	171.5: *gcig*	
9c	53.6: *ji*	172.2: **de**	TR prefers KTL
9d	53.6: **mthug**	172.4: *thug*	TR prefers RT
10a	53.6: *ba lang*	176.6: **ba glang**	TR prefers KTL
10b	53.7: **skam**	173.1: *skams*	
10d	53.7: **yang na**	missing in 173.2–173.3	
10d	53.7: **skam**	173.3: *skams*	

11a	53.7: *tsha*	175.2: *tshwa*	
11b	53.7: *dngar*	175.3: *mngar*	TR prefers KTL
12c	54.1: *'brug*	missing in 176.5	
12c	54.1: *sngangs*	176.5: *dngangs*	TR prefers KTL
13a	54.1: *tha ma*	177.3: *mtha' ma*	
13b	54.2: *tha ma*	177.5: *mtha' ma*	
13c	54.2: *du*	177.6: *tu*	
13c	54.2: *rtog*	177.6: *rtogs*	TR prefers RT
13d	54.2: *pas so*	178.4: *yin no*	
15a	54.3: *ngos kyi*	182.1: *ngos su*	TR prefers KTL
15d	54.3: *bdan*	182.4: *bden*	
16b	54.4: *du*	183.3: *tu*	
16c	54.4: *gyis*	183.4: *gyi*	
17b	54.4: *ltar*	184.1: *su*	
17d	54.5: *du*	184.2: *tu*	
21a	54.6: *su*	187.6: *ni*	
21c	54.6: *gang zhig*	188.1: *de ni*	TR prefers KTL
22b	55.1: *bas*	189.3: *byas*	TR prefers KTL
23a	55.1: *ni*	missing in 190.1	
24a	55.2: *kha cig tsangs ba'i gnas su 'od spar nas*	109.3–4: *kha cig 'od spar na tshangs pa'i gnas su*	
25d	55.3: *rin cher*	191.3: *rin po che*	RT corrected to *rin chen*
25c & d			The order is reversed in KTL
27a	55.4: *e bam*	193.2: *e vam*	TR prefers KTL
27d	55.4: *zhes pa*	195.1: *zhen pa*	
28b	55.5: *rgyug par*	195.1: *brgyug*	
28c	55.5: *ngoms*	195.6: *nus*	TR prefers KTL
28c	55.5: *'ching*	195.6: *'chi*	
29b	55.5: *dang*	196.6: *gang*	TR prefers KTL

30c	55.6: *chugs*	199.3: **gos**	
31a	55.7: **blta**	199.6: *lta*	
31c	55.7: *brtan*	200.2: **bstan**	
31c	55.7: *'ching*	200.3: *'chang*	
33a	56.1: **de**	201.6: *de'i*	
33b	56.1: **dag**	202.2: *dang*	
33d	56.2: **de**	202.4: *de'i*	
34b	56.2: *blo mi*	203.3: *blo'i*	corrected to **yi**
35b	56.3: **de**	204.2: *'di*	
36a	56.3: **du mas**	204.5: *du ma*	
36c	56.4: **bsgom**	205.3: *sgom*	
36c	56.4: *bstan*	205.3: **brtan**	TR prefers KTL
36d	56.4: **bdag nyid**	205.3: *bdag gis*	
36c & d	56.3–4: *gsal ba gang zhig shes pa bsgom pa brtan / mi g.yo'i sems ni bdag nyid de ru gzung*	205.2–3: *gsal ba gang zhig mi g.yo ba'i shes pa / sgom brtan sems ni bdag gis de ru gzung*	Translation follows KTL
37b	56.4: *mthong ba'i*	205.6: **mthong bas**	
37c	56.4: *bros*	206.1: **phros**	
37c	56.4: **med**	205.6: *min*	
38a	56.4: **dang**	206.4: *ste*	
38b	56.4: **skyed**	206.5: *skye*	
38b	56.4: *sti*	missing	corrected to *ste*
39d	56.5: **ni**	208.3: *pa*	
40c	56.6: **dag**	209.4: *gang*	

Appendix 4

Some Reflections on *Dran med*

The translation of the Tibetan term *dran (pa) med (pa)* (pronounced "drenmay") presents an interesting complexity. As a standard form of negation, *med pa* is rather easily translated: it usually means "not" "without," "nonexistent," or "there is/are none of." *Dran pa*, however, is challenging, as it has a wide range of meaning, clustered around the two terms "memory" and "mindfulness." These meanings can include: "recollecting," "memorizing," "being mindful of," "recognition," "remembering," "holding in mind," "consideration," "thinking about," "missing someone or something," and "pay attention to." The particular translation that is chosen from all of these possibilities depends on the context in which *dran pa* or *dran med* appears.

The term *dran med* itself has a long history. An early instance of its rise to prominence was in eighth-century Tibet during the critical and still-discussed debate between Kamalaśīla from India and Hwa Shang Mahayana from China. According to the Tibetan tradition, there were two main points in contention: whether good deeds were necessary to attain enlightenment and whether thoughts should be obliterated or not.

It is said that Hwa Shang advocated the eradication of all discursive thinking and emphasized a practice that led to the absence of mental activity. In Tibetan, the terms used in the debate were *yid la mi byed pa* (Skt. *amanasikāra*) or *dran med* (Skt. *asmṛti*), which David Ruegg has translated respectively as "non-mentation" and "non-minding."[55] In the context of Hwa Shang's reported position, these terms are pushed to their extreme to mean elimination of all thought processes, whether good or bad. This would mean that with no thoughts, there are no deeds, no good actions in the world, and no accumulation of merit. According to Kamalaśila, however, what is meant by non-mentation is not just an absence of mentation; the term implies the lack of objectification and the nonfunctioning of ordinary apprehension, both of which are experienced by someone whose prajñā is engaged in analysis.[56]

Matthew Kapstein also notes the bi-valence of the term. In discussing the views of a dzogchen master, Kapstein translates *dran pa* as "mnemonic engagement" and *dran med* as "amnesis" or a lack of mindfulness, which is active in "constituting the bewilderment of samsara." He notes, however, that in terms of practicing the path, *dran med* can also mean "freedom from discursive thought."[57] With this meaning in mind, he quotes the master again: "Mnemic engagement is the ground; amnesis is the path…. Mnemic engagement is appearance; amnesis is emptiness…."[58] Here, *dran med* is equated with the path and with emptiness.

Herbert Guenther translates *dran pa* as "memory" and *dran med* as "non-memory," though he hastens to say that this translation "should not be confused with the usual associations the word *memory* carries for us."[59] He sets the terms, which he understands to have an inbuilt tension between them, in a dynamic discussion of "wholeness transcending the pale of the ego-centered mind that 'grasps' whatever it fancies there 'to be grasped' and at the same time invites us to cultivate a visionary capacity and joyful ecstasy."[60] Throughout his extended discussion of the term *dran med*, Guenther almost always prefers to leave the term in Tibetan, which leads one to believe that he is not very satisfied with "non-memory" as a translation. And, despite his protestations, it is indeed difficult to shake the connotation of bringing up the past.

Now let us turn to Saraha. As did Kamalaśila, Saraha used the term *dran med* not on the superficial level of absence of thought but more deeply. In verse 30, he describes *dran med* as mind "completely purified of the afflictions"; like the utpala flower in a swamp, it is "not affected by the faults arising from samsara nor by the qualities found in the Victorious Ones." In *A Song for the People*, he states that at the stage of *dran med*, "apprehending 'I' and 'mine' is forgotten."[61] Here, *dran med* refers to a state beyond the afflictions and beyond the self.

Karma Trinlépa glosses *dran med* as nonmentation, or "resting in the absence of mental activity."[62] He gives it profound significance when discussing Saraha's four symbols by setting up the following correlations: (1) among the four joys, *dran med* corresponds to supreme joy, understood as seeing that mindfulness and the nature of mind are emptiness; (2) among the four seals, it is the wisdom seal, understood as seeing the emptiness of mind's nature; and (3) among the four samādhis, it is the samādhi of the lion's play, understood as seeing that relative appearances have no true existence and that mindfulness, like a powerful lion, overcomes all mental afflictions.

In his oral commentary on *A Song for the King*, Thrangu Rinpoche underlined the ultimate meaning of the term. On verse 29, he comments that *dran med* "does not mean that we lose the faculty of mindfulness; rather, it means seeing the nature of mind, seeing the emptiness of even mindfulness itself." On verse 27, he explains that it points to a time when the mind has come to rest and then one "is able to recognize the emptiness of mindfulness itself." From this perspective, mindfulness corresponds to śamatha practice when the mind is calmed, and *dran med* to vipaśyanā when the nature of the mind is seen. Finally, concerning verse 33, Thrangu Rinpoche describes *dran med* as "mindfulness dissolved into the expanse beyond mindfulness."

How then to translate *dran med*? Traleg Kyabgon Rinpoche suggested "mindfulness of nonmindfulness," which captures many of the meanings, but it is a bit cumbersome for verse. Other possibilities are: *release/d from mindfulness*, which was sometimes used in the translation in the sense of letting go of a mind engaged in thinking on a relative level; *beyond mindfulness*, which moves too far away from mindfulness, for the emptiness of mindfulness itself must be allowed for; and *absence of mindfulness* or *without mindfulness,* which enforce too strong a negation, for as Thrangu Rinpoche noted, *dran med* does not mean that we lose the faculty of mindfulness. Finally, it seemed that *nonminding* caught the widest range of meaning while not excluding deeper levels. In *Merriam Webster's Collegiate Dictionary, Eleventh Edition,* "to mind" can mean "to consider important" and "to be concerned about." Its negation would imply a lack of concern or importance, and this relates directly to Saraha's indication that *dran med* means that one forgets the self: concerns about "I" and "mine" are dropped. As in the statement, "I don't mind," there's an indifference to the dramas of the self. Further, *The New Shorter Oxford English Dictionary* lists many meanings for "to mind" that correspond to mindfulness: "remember," "recollect," "bear in mind," "pay attention to," and "notice." In this context, *nonminding* would mean not engaging in ordinary thinking—not being caught by the conceptualizing that binds us to the relative world—which then allows for the realization of the deeper truth, the seeing of mind's empty nature.

Even if one could find the perfect English term that corresponds exactly to the Tibetan, it would not be possible to convey all the levels and dynamics of meaning that are implied by *dran med.* As with so many of the terms in Buddhism—emptiness, dependent arising, and no self, to name a few—the full range of meaning can be understood only through study. Indeed, it is possible to argue that research into Buddhism could be condensed into discussions of these terms.

Notes

1 The most comprehensive study to date of Saraha is Kurtis Schaeffer's excellent *Dreaming the Great Brahmin: Tibetan Traditions of the Buddhist Poet-Saint Saraha* (New York: Oxford University Press, 2005). The text also contains a translation of Saraha's *A Song for the People* along with commentary.

For an insightful look at the cultural and scholarly background for Saraha's spiritual songs, see: Roger R. Jackson, *Tantric Treasures: Three Collections of Mystical Verse from Buddhist India* (New York: Oxford University Press, 2004). The book contains an annotated translation of *A Song for the People* and a useful abstract of themes found in all the songs: "(1) a rhetoric of paradox, (2) cultural critique, (3) focus on the innate, (4) affirmation of the body, the senses, and sexuality, (5) the promotion of certain yogic techniques, and (6) celebration of the guru." p. 16.

2 For early mahāmudrā, see George N. Roerich, *The Blue Annals* (Delhi: Motilal Banarsidass, 1976), esp. pp. 839ff.

3 Schaeffer, *Dreaming the Great Brahmin*, p. 86.

4 *Do ha skor gsum ti ka 'bring po sems kyi rnam thar ston pa'i me long* (Kunzang Tobgyel, Thimphu, Bhutan: Druk Sherig Press, 1984), f. 135.1–4.

5 With interpolations from Karma Trinlépa's commentary in brackets, the complete verse reads:

> The four letters, which [are the means] to accomplish [the supreme siddhi, indicate the four stages: mindfulness, nonminding, the unborn, and beyond the intellect].
> Among these, I first teach [mindfulness].
> As you drink the elixir [of nonminding, apprehending] "I" [and "mine"] is forgotten.
> Whoever [realizes that mind itself is forever unborn will come] to know the reality of the single letter [*A*, the unborn].
> [Ultimately beyond the intellect], the [nature of mind] knows neither name [nor symbol].

> *Sgrub yig bzhi las dang po bdag gis ston / khu ba 'thungs bas nga ni brjed bar gyur / gang gis yi ge gcig shes pa / de yis ming ni mi shes so.* Saraha, *Dohakoshagiti. Do ha mdzod gyi glu* (Delhi: *sDe-dge Bstan-'gyur.* Delhi Karmapae Chodhey Gyalwae Sungrab Partun Khang, 1982–1985), *Rgyud 'grel,* (D2224), vol. Wi., f. 76.1.

> "The four letters" refer to E Vam Ma Ya, which is the fourth level of interpretation given by Karma Trinlépa.

6 *Spro pa phyi nas gcod dang nang nas gcod / lta ba'i stong lugs mi gcig man na yang / thab kyi me bsad du ba 'gags pa ltar / nang du rang sems rtsa ba gcod pa zab.* Karma chags med, *'Phags pa thugs rje chen po'i dmar khrid phyag rdzogs zung 'jugs gi nyams len snying po bsdus pa.* From *Gdam ngag mdzod* (Delhi: Sechen Publications, 1999), ff. 327.5–328.1.

7 These four stages are presented sequentially by Karma Trinlépa in his commentary on *A Song for the People*. However, in *A Song for the King*, Saraha reverses the first two stages, so that nonminding comes first, followed by mindfulness. In this way, we are given at the outset a taste of what it is to be free of the afflictions, and then we return to the first stage to establish a more stable and tranquil mind.

8 The four yogas are described by the Ninth Karmapa, Wangchuk Dorjé, in his texts on the practice of mahāmudrā. For detailed discussion, see the Dbang phyug rdor rje, Rgyal dbang Ka rma pa, *Lhan cig skyes sbyor gyi zab khrid nges don rgya mtsho'i snying po phrin las 'od 'phro* (Rumtek, Sikkim: Dharma Chakra Centre, n.d.); *Mahamudra: The Ocean of Definitive Meaning*, trans. Elizabeth M. Callahan (Seattle: Nitartha International, 2001), pp. 211–46; Khenchen Thrangu Rinpoche, *Essentials of Mahamudra: Looking Directly at the Mind* (Boston: Wisdom Publications, 2004), pp. 242–49.

9 For example, *Mahamudra* and *Clarifying the Natural State* by Dakpo Tashi Namgyal and the three great commentaries on mahāmudrā by the Ninth Karmapa, Wangchuk Dorjé: *The Ocean of Definitive Meaning, Eliminating the Darkness of Ignorance*, and *Pointing Out the Dharmakaya*. See the bibliography for Thrangu Rinpoche's commentaries on these texts.

10 The short lineage passes from Tilopa to Nāropa, Marpa, Milarepa, Gampopa, and then to the First Karmapa, Düsum Khyenpa, down to the present Seventeenth Karmapa, Ogyen Trinley Dorjé.

11 The long lineage passes from Śākyamuni Buddha to Saraha, Nāgārjuna, Shavari, Maitripa, Marpa and then continues the same as the short lineage down to the present Karmapa, Ogyen Trinley Dorjé.

12 These are discussed in greater detail in the commentary on the four symbols beginning with verse 29.

13 *mda'* is Tibetan for "arrow" and *brda'* is Tibetan for "symbol."

14 For a version of this text plus scholarly commentary on its history and on Saraha himself, see Herbert V. Guenther, tr., *The Royal Song of Saraha: A Study in the History of Buddhist Thought* (Seattle: University of Washington Press, 1969; Taiwan: SMC Publishing, 1992). This translation is reprised in Herbert V. Guenther, tr. *Ecstatic Spontaneity: Saraha's Three Cycles of Doha* (Fremont, CA: Asian Humanities Press, 1993).

15 "How things really are," or "abiding reality" (Tib. *gnas lugs*) is paired with "how they appear," or "apparent reality" (Tib. *snang lugs*). They belong to sets of terms in which one element relates to the ultimate level and the other to the relative, such as emptiness and appearance, the definitive and the provisional, and so forth.

16 *phyag rgya chen po.*

17 An etymology given at the beginning of a text or discussion is often focused more on presenting the condensed meaning of the whole text than on the usual tracing of a term's linguistic origin.

18 *phyag 'tshal ba.*

19 *phyag ma.*

20 *Gsal ba* is also translated as "cognizance," since it refers to the mind's ability to know. The related term *'od bsal* is translated variously as "radiant clarity," "cognitive lucidity," or "luminosity." It is also paired with emptiness to indicate that *empty* does not mean a void or vacuum: it is the unceasing source of all appearance and all knowing.

21 A synonym for *doha* in Tibetan is *rdo rje mgur*, "vajra song." For an excellent discussion of the origins of the doha and their language of Apabhramsa, see Schaeffer, *Dreaming the Great Brahmin*, esp. chap. 4.

22 Mañjuśrī is the deity who embodies wisdom, and so he is often supplicated by the translator at the beginning of a text.

23 The *Heart Sutra* belongs to a corpus of texts known as the Prajñāpāramitā sutras, which form the core of the texts for the Buddha's middle turning of the wheel of Dharma. These sutras emphasized: the empty nature of phenomena; the development of the wisdom to see this reality; and the compassion to devote one's life to benefiting others.

24 For a complete translation, see "The Song of Lodro Thaye" in *The Rain of Wisdom*, trans. Nālandā Translation Committee (Boston: Shambhala Publications, 1980), pp. 81–90. The line Thrangu Rinpoche discusses is found on p. 83: "There are both things as they are and the way of confusion."

25 "Adventitious" here means that the confusion is separate from the nature of the mind, which remains pure and untouched by the delusion that makes up samsara. Since this bewilderment is not a part of mind itself, it can be removed through study, reflection, and meditation.

26 This follows the commentary rather than the root verse, which runs: *ji ltar rmongs pas bzlog nas bltas pa yis,* "The ignorant look with their eyes rolled back."

27 *Don sphyi,* also translated as "generic image," refers to the mental image we create that is abstracted from our experience of numerous instances of an object.

28 *Sgra spyi,* also translated as "generic sound," refers to any verbal convention, which can be applied to any object and therefore has no essential link to it. This becomes obvious when you think about a woman who is named Rose. Ordinary perception can be understood as a fusing of the generic image and the generic sound, happening so quickly that we are not aware of it and think that we are seeing an actual object that is indeed the name it is called.

29 The reasoning of *one and many* is one of the main logical tools of the Middle Way. First, an object is analyzed to see that it is not one thing; for example, you see that even atoms have sides and directions and therefore are not unitary. Having proven that an object is not one thing, then an accumulation of these could not be any more real than the one thing that did not exist. Another famous reasoning is called the Diamond Slivers, which demonstrates a phenomenon to be free of arising through showing that it does not arise from itself, from another, from self and other combined, nor from a negation of this combination. The reasoning of dependent arising shows that phenomena come about through the gathering of various causes and conditions and therefore do not ultimately exist. These three reasonings belong to the famous five reasonings of the Middle Way.

30 One of the five texts by Maitreya through Asanga, *The Ornament of Clear Realization* is a subtle presentation of meditative states and the Prajñāpāramitā sutras. See Khenchen Thrangu Rinpoche, *The Ornament of Clear Realization: A Commentary on the Prajanaparamita by Maitreya* (Crestone, CO: Namo Buddha Publications and Auckland: Zhyisil Chokyi Ghatsal Charitable Trust Publications, 2004).

31 These last two lines give another example that illustrates the absence of increase and decrease. Karma Trinlépa explains that ultimately, the radiance of the great sphere is unceasing; within its vastness, living beings of the six realms take birth and pass away. In relation to this process, one should not understand taking birth as being a thing (some real entity) and passing away as a nonthing (the absence of a real entity). The perspective in these examples from verses 5 and 6 is that of a system taken as a whole. Karma 'phrin las pa, *Do ha skor gsum ti ka 'bring po sems kyi*

rnam thar ston pa'i me long. (Kunzang Tobgyel, Thimphu, Bhutan: Druk Sherig Press, 1984), f. 169.

32 *Supreme Continuum* by Maitreya through Asanga. The longer Sanskrit titles are: *Mahāyānottaratantraśāstra* or *Ratnagotravibhanga.* It was translated into Tibetan as *Theg pa chen po rgyud bla ma bstan bcos* (Toh. 4024). The text has been translated into English several times. Rosie Fuchs, tr., *Buddha Nature: The Mahayana Uttaratantra Shastra by Arya Maitreya with Commentary by Jamgon Kongtrul Lodro Thaye, "The Unassailable Lion's Roar," and Explanations by Khenpo Tsultrim Gyamtso Rinpoche* (Ithaca, NY: Snow Lion Publications, 2000); Ken Holmes, *Maitreya on Buddha Nature* (Forres, Scotland: Altea Publishing, 1999).

33 Incongruent, or contradictory, means that the analogy shows what we should not do or what the nature is not. Congruent, or noncontradictory, means that the analogy shows what we should do or alludes to what the nature is.

34 A classic example is the chariot (analogous to the present-day automobile). Until it is broken down into its parts, we might think there is something called "a chariot." But if each part is examined, it is obvious that a particular part is not the chariot and we have simply imputed the concept "chariot" onto a collection of parts.

35 Passed from teacher to student, oral or "key" instructions describe how to practice. Even though many have been written down, they retain the lively and succinct quality of a personal encounter.

36 Karma Trinlépa comments, regarding "First a thing and in the end a nonthing," that you might think, "Spontaneously present, primordial wisdom first arises as a thing and then in the end passes away, turning into a nonthing." This type of thinking, however, creates an inherent nature both in appearance and in emptiness. Primordial wisdom, however, is unitary and not established as the duality of a thing and nonthing. Then again, primordial wisdom is not other than these two; it is not *not* these two. Karma 'phrin las pa, f. 177.

    Karma Trinlépa presents the argument in this way to counteract two extreme views. His first point counteracts taking something to be permanent through possessing an inherent nature, and this is refuted. His second point counteracts taking something to be annihilated by affirming that primordial wisdom is not other than these two.

37 An alternative translation of the last two lines: "Likewise, those who [enter] the circle of the mandala / Through the formless nature will know [uninterrupted meditation]." "The circle of the mandala" refers to the central figure of the mandala along with the related deities.

38 This statement may seem to be a paradox but it is based on two main factors: (1) not recognizing the empty nature of all appearances, including oneself, and (2) the powerful, ingrained habits of perception that reinforce a way of seeing that is mistaken. These two taken together create a misapprehension that is vivid. In commenting on this verse, Karma Trinlépa notes that conceptualization itself is ignorance and cultivating that ignorance makes it clearer. Karma 'phrin las pa, f. 185.

39 Following the explanations of the Third Karmapa, Rangjung Dorjé, most Kagyü lamas follow a system of analyzing the mind into eight types of consciousness. The five types of sensory consciousness (visual, aural, olfactory, gustatory, and tactile) are nonconceptual and function to gather raw data. The sixth (mental) consciousness integrates this information and can also create concepts. The seventh (afflicted) consciousness is a continuous sense of "I" that filters experience in terms of one's sense of self. The

eighth consciousness, also called the ālaya or all-basis consciousness, has two functions: It stores impressions from the consciousnesses related to the sense faculties and it also gives rise to habitual patterns that cause thought and activity. There are other schools of thought that accept only the first six consciousnesses and not the seventh and eighth.

40 This refers to advanced practices with a consort.

41 This line refers to the practice of *tummo* (Tib. *gtum mo;* Skt. *caṇḍālī*), "inner heat." "Space" indicates emptiness. According to Karma Trinlépa's commentary, "it" refers to the concentrated subtle energy that falls from the letter *Haṃ* visualized in the crown. The faults are clinging to this passing experience of bliss and, further, the illness that follows from that attachment. Karma 'phrin las pa, f. 189.

42 These subtle energies are associated with completion stage practices and the six yogas of Nāropa.

43 Also known as the *Collection of Select Sayings*. In Sanskrit, it is *Udānavarga* and in Tibetan, *Ched du brjod pa'i tshoms* (Toh. 326).

44 Defiled virtue refers to positive actions that are performed by someone who is still caught within a world of dualistic perception. This means that there is consciousness of a subject and an object, a doer of the deed and a deed to be done.

45 Another explanation relates to an esoteric technique involving the interaction of the tongue and the smaller tongue, which refers to the uvula.

46 *rang rig* in Tibetan, also translated as "reflexive awareness."

47 *rang rig pa'i ye shes* in Tibetan, also translated as "primordial wisdom aware of its own nature."

48 Karma Trinlépa gives extensive commentary here, noting for example that *E* is the expanse of beyond mindfulness and *Vam* arises from it as a mere emanation. On the simplest level, he states that through analogies and their meanings, the reality of the letters *E Vam* can be correctly understood. Karma 'phrin las pa, f. 193.

49 "Mindfulness" and "recollection" both translate the Tibetan term *dran pa.* "Alertness" translates *shes bzhin*, which also comes into English as "attentiveness," "watchfulness," "conscientiousness," and "vigilance." For discussions of memory and mindfulness, see Janet Gyatso, ed., *In the Mirror of Memory: Reflections on Mindfulness and Remembrance in Indian and Tibetan Buddhism* (Albany: State University of New York Press, 1992).

50 For an extended discussion of nonminding, see appendix 4, "Some Reflections on *Dran med.*"

51 In his commentary on the *Prayer of Maitreya*, Mendon Tshampa Rinpoche gives commentary on three of these four samādhis in Mendon Tshampa Rinpoche, *The Prayer of Maitreya and an Easy Path to Enlightenment: A Short Commentary on the Aspiration Prayer of Maitreya*, trans. Michele Martin (Kathmandu: Marpa Institute for Translators, 1996), pp. 38–39.

52 For an explanation of the four joys, see the commentary to verse 27.

53 See footnote 26.

54 In this edition of the text, verse 37 is only three lines.

55 David Seyfort Ruegg, *Buddha-nature, Mind and the Problem of Gradualism in a Comparative Perspective: On the Transmission and Reception of Buddhism in India and Tibet* (New Delhi: Heritage Publishers, 1992), p. 99.

56 *Ibid.*, p. 94.

57 Matthew Kapstein, "The Amnesic Monarch," in Gyatso, pp. 246–47.

58 *Ibid.*, p. 267, fn. 24.

59 Guenther, *Ecstatic Spontaneity,* p. 38.
60 *Ibid.*, p. 40.
61 See the discussion in the Editor's Introduction.
62 *De nas yid la mi byed pa'i ngang du 'jog pa dran med kyi kho ba 'thung.* Karma 'phrin las pa, *Do ha skor gsum,* f. 76.2.

Glossary

afflicted consciousness. *See* eight consciousnesses

afflictions. *See* disturbing emotions

aggregate (*skandha*, Skt.; *phung po,* Tib.). The aggregates are the constituents of our mental and physical life. The five are: form, sensation, discrimination, mental formation, and consciousness.

ālaya consciousness. *See* eight consciousnesses

bodhicitta (Skt.; *byang chub kyi sems,* Tib.). In general, this "mind of awakening" is the motivation to attain full awakening so that one can bring others to that same liberation. It is divided into ultimate bodhi-citta, which is the realization of mind's nature, and relative bodhi-citta, which is again divided into the aspiration and the actual engagement in the practice of the six or ten perfections.

bodhisattva (Skt.; *byang chub sems dpa'*, Tib.). The Tibetan means a "hero of enlightenment." Bodhisattvas are those who have dedicated their lives to the realization of mind's nature and to compassionate action in order to help others on the path to liberation. The term refers both to individuals on the Mahayana path and to those who have achieved a high level of realization and abide on the bodhisattva levels, such as Avalokiteśvara, the embodiment of compassion, and Mañjuśrī, the embodiment of wisdom.

bodhisattva levels (*bhūmi*, Skt.; *sa,* Tib.). The ten successive grounds or stages of a bodhisattva's practice, beginning with the initial realization of emptiness on the first level and culminating with the vajralike samādhi at the end of the tenth level opening into full realization. On each level, there are defects to be discarded and qualities to be manifested.

buddha nature (*tathāgatagarbha*, Skt.; *de bzhin gshegs pa'i snying po,* Tib.). A synonym for the ultimate nature of mind, which emphasizes its stainless quality and its presence within all living beings as their primordial nature. While a practitioner moves along the path to full awakening, this nature becomes increasingly apparent until it is fully revealed and manifest at the final stage of enlightenment.

Cakrasaṃvara (Skt.; *'Khor lo sdom pa,* Tib.). A semiwrathful male deity and the principal practice of the mother tantras. This is one of the five main practices in the Kagyü lineage.

channels, winds, and drops (*nāḍi, prāṇa, bindu,* Skt.; *rtsa, rlung, thig le,* Tib.). These are aspects of the subtle physical body. The channels are pathways through which the winds, or currents of energy, flow. The drops, or spheres, ride on the winds.

coemergent wisdom (*sahajajñāna,* Skt.; *lhan cig skyes pa'i ye shes,* Tib.). This term highlights the fact that wisdom arises together with ignorance; in other words, nirvana is simultaneous with samsara. All four terms have the same nature; seeing them as different comes from not recognizing this.

completion stage (*sampannakrama,* Skt.; *rdzogs rim,* Tib.). The second phase of visualization practice, which follows the generation stage. All the conceptualized images are dissolved back into the emptiness whence they came. More subtly, this stage can be divided into an aspect that has features, referring to the practice of channels, winds, and drops, and an aspect without features, referring to the practice of mahāmudrā. *See also* generation stage

ḍākinī (Skt.; *mkha' 'dro ma,* Tib.). A feminine figure who ranges in meaning from a worldly deity with a variety of functions to an enlightened embodiment of wisdom. As one of the three roots (guru, yidam, and ḍākinī) in the Vajrayāna, she is known as the source of activity.

Dakpo Tashi Namgyal (*Dwags po Bkra shis rnam rgyal,* 1512–87). A great Tibetan teacher who functioned as Gampopa's regent, Tashi Namgyal is famous for his text known as *Moonbeams of Mahamudra* (translated into English as *Mahamudra: The Quintessence of Mind and Meditation*), in which he combines discussions of view and instructions on meditation into a manual that is also a treasury of quotations from philosophical treatises and advice on how to practice.

denial (*skur 'deps,* Tib.). Literally, "to hurl abuse" in Tibetan, the term means to assume as nonexistent what does exist, for example, a self on the relative level. The term is also translated as "derogation" or "denigration." *See also* superimposition

dharmadhātu (Skt.; *chos dbyings,* Tib.). The expanse of all phenomena, a synonym for ultimate reality. It points to what the master Tilopa states in *Mahamudra, The Ocean of Definitive Meaning:* "From time without beginning, the true nature of mind is like space./There is no phenomenon that is not included therein."

dharmakāya. *See* kāyas

dharmatā (Skt.; *chos nyid,* Tib.). Reality itself, another synonym for the ultimate, often used to indicate its presence as the empty nature of all phenomena, in other words, as embedded or enfolded within relative truth. *See also* two truths

disturbing emotions (*kleśa,* Skt.; *nyon mongs,* Tib.). Among the different mental events, the disturbing emotions are listed as the six root afflictions of ignorance, aversion, excessive desire, pride, doubt, and wrong view. They are also presented as the five mental and emotional afflictions of ignorance, aversion, excessive desire, pride, and envy; these can be condensed into the three poisons of ignorance, aversion, and excessive desire.

doha (Skt. and Tib.). A spiritual song sprung from the deep experience of a realized practitioner. The tradition can be traced back to the mahāsiddhas of the eighth to the twelfth centuries in India and to its most famous Tibetan exponent, Milarepa. The term is synonymous with "vajra song" (*rdo rje glu,* Tib.).

eight consciousnesses (*aṣṭavijñāna,* Skt.; *rnam shes brgyad,* Tib.). Mental processing can be divided into eight aspects. Five consciousnesses are associated with the five sense faculties, known as visual, auditory, olfactory, gustatory, and tactile. The sixth (mental) consciousness operates with the data provided by the five sense faculties. The seventh (afflicted) consciousness interprets experience in terms of a personal self. The eighth, or all-basis, consciousness has two functions: it stores the traces of habitual patterns and, when the conditions are right, gives rise to them.

exaggeration. *See* superimposition

father tantra (*pha rgyud,* Tib.). This aspect of tantric practice emphasizes skillful means. The generation stage practices focus on male deities, and the completion stage practice accentuates the illusory body.

Foundational Vehicle (*hīnayāna,* Skt.; *theg pa dman pa,* Tib.). In the Tibetan context, it is understood as the part of the Buddhist heritage that focuses on the rules and regulations for the ordained sangha and on the practice of liberating oneself from the ocean of samsara. In general usage, the term often overlaps with Theravada, "the school of the elders," which is still practiced in Thailand, Burma, Sri Lanka, Laos, and Cambodia.

four joys (*dga' ba bzhi,* Tib.). As joy passes down the central channel in increasing levels of subtlety, the four are known as: (1) *joy,* joined with seeing the illusory nature of phenomena; (2) *supreme joy,* joined with seeing mindfulness and the nature of mind to be empty; (3) *without joy,* joined to freedom from attachment to joy; and (4) *coemergent joy,* which is beyond the intellect. These joys become part of the path when the practices of the subtle winds and channels are performed in concert with the recognition of mind's nature.

four seals (*mudrā,* Skt.; *phyag rgya,* Tib.). In the context of Saraha's doha, they refer to the seal of phenomena, the seal of wisdom, the seal of commitment, and the great seal. They are correlated with the four symbols, the four joys, and the four samādhis.

four stages. *See* four symbols

four symbols (*brda' bzhi,* Tib.). A system of stages in the realization of mahāmudrā that is unique to Saraha. The first stage is mindfulness, followed by nonminding, the unborn, and beyond the intellect. See verses 29 to 33 and their commentary for an explanation. For a discussion of nonminding, see Appendix 4.

Gampopa (*Sgam po pa,* 1079–1153). He began his practice in the Kadampa tradition of Atiśa and then blended its focus on ethical behavior and a graduated path of practice together with the mahāmudrā instructions he received from Milarepa. Gampopa was one of Milarepa's two main disciples and founded the Kagyü monastic tradition. He also wrote *The Ornament of Precious Liberation,* a comprehensive text on philosophy and meditation that is still widely studied.

generation stage (*utpattikrama,* Skt.; *bskyed rim,* Tib.). The first phase of visualization practice, in which the deity, arising out of emptiness, is brought to mind in vivid detail as a central focus while the deity's mantra is recited. *See also* completion stage

guru yoga (*bla ma'i rnal 'byor,* Tib.). Among the three roots of the guru, yidam, and ḍākinī, the guru is considered the source of blessings. The practice of guru yoga develops a deep connection with the teacher, which allows these blessings to flow as the mind of the disciple blends with the mind of the root teacher, who is seen as the embodiment of all buddhas. Guru yoga is the fourth and last of the special preliminary practices.

Hevajra (Skt.; *kye rdo rje,* Tib.). This semiwrathful male deity is an important practice in the Kagyü and Sakya traditions and was the main yidam of Marpa the Translator. The condensed version of this tantra along with the Third Karmapa, Rangjung Dorjé's *Profound Inner Meaning* and Maitreya's *Supreme Continuum* are considered the three major texts for practitioners in the Gyalwang Karmapa's tradition.

inner heat (*caṇḍālī,* Skt.; *gtum mo,* Tib.). A practice of the subtle body which generates internal heat to burn up obscurations and confusion. One of the six yogas of Nāropa.

Jamgön Kongtrül Lodrö Tayé (*'Jam mgon kong sprul blo gros mtha' yas,* 1813–99). One of Tibet's great masters of meditation and scholarship, he played a central role in the nineteenth-century renaissance of Tibetan spirituality, known as the rimé, or nonsectarian, movement. His work helped to preserve many traditions in Tibet that were on the verge of extinction. Jamgön Kongtrül's most famous texts were known as the Five Treasuries.

Kagyü (*bka' brgyud,* Tib.). "The Lineage of Oral Transmission"; one of the four major schools of Tibetan Buddhism (the others are the Nyingma, Sakya, and Gelug). It emphasizes the practice of meditation and, in particular, mahāmudrā.

Karma Trinlépa (*Karma 'phrin las pa,* 1456–1539). A Kagyü poet and scholar, his extensive commentary on Saraha's trilogy of doha elucidates the deeper levels of meaning in the Songs for the People, the Queen, and the King and also serves as the primary source for a Tibetan history of Saraha's verses. Karma Trinlépa was the teacher of the Eighth Karmapa, Mikyö Dorjé.

Karmapa (*Karma pa,* Tib.). His name means "The One of Buddha's Activity" and he is also seen as the embodiment of compassion. His second incarnation was recognized as the first tulku in Tibet, beginning a lineage that has included illustrious scholars, masters of meditation, and artists; it has continued down to the present day with his seventeenth incarnation, the Gyalwang Karmapa, Ogyen Trinley Dorjé.

kāyas (Skt.; *sku,* Tib.). In the Mahayana, full awakening is often described in terms of the kāyas, meaning "bodies" or "dimensions of reality," which number two, three, four, or five. When they are two, they are the dharmakāya (dimension or body of truth) and the rūpakāya (body of form). The dharmakāya is the perfect realization of mind's nature and replete with enlightened qualities; it is nonconceptual and synonymous with emptiness or omniscience. When the kāyas are three, the rūpakāya is divided into the sambhogakāya (body of bliss or enjoyment) and the nirmāṇakāya (body of manifestation or emanation). Expressing the nature of radiant clarity, the sambhogakāya is visible only to bodhisattvas on the ten levels. It is adorned with the major and minor marks and further defined through the five certainties of time, place, teacher, retinue, and teaching. The nirmāṇakāya is the fully awakened mind that manifests without impediment in a variety of forms and remains visible to ordinary beings; Śākyamuni Buddha is an example of a nirmāṇakāya. When the kāyas are four, the svābhāvikakāya (body of the essential nature) refers to the inseparability of the other three. When the kāyas are five, the mahāsukhakāya (body of great bliss) refers to the blissful nature of the dharmakāya. See verse 38 for Saraha's version of the five kāyas.

lucidity (*ābhāsvara,* Skt.; *'od gsal,* Tib.). Also translated as "radiant clarity" and "luminosity," the term refers to the ability of the mind to know, a quality that is utterly inseparable from its empty nature.

mahāmudrā (Skt.; *phya rgya chen po,* Tib.). The Great *(maha)* Seal *(mudra)* is the supreme practice in the Kagyü lineage. Its practices lead to a recognition of the nature of the mind, which is often defined as the union of bliss and emptiness. Describing this practice in *The Ocean of Definitive Meaning,* the great Indian adept Maitripa (1012–97) states: "All phenomena are empty of self-essence. / The mind grasping them as empty is purified into its ground. / Free of intellect, with no object for the mind, / This is the path of all Buddhas."

mahāsiddha. *See* siddha

Mahayana (*mahāyāna,* Skt.; *theg pa chen po,* Tib.). The "Great Vehicle" is a further development of Buddhist thought and practice based on the Foundational Vehicle, and focusing on compassion and emptiness. It is also known as the path of the bodhisattva. It can be divided into the Pāramitāyāna (the Vehicle of the Perfections) and the Vajrayāna. Without its Vajrayāna component, it is found mainly in China, Korea, and Japan. Within the system of Tibetan Buddhism, it is the second of three vehicles— Hinayana, Mahayana, and Vajrayana—and is understood to function as the basis of the Vajrayana view and practice.

Maitreya (Skt.; *byams pa,* Tib.). As the next and fifth buddha, Maitreya resides in Tuṣita Heaven. It is from him that Asaṅga received what are known as the Five Treatises of Maitreya. These constitute an important corpus of texts for the Buddhist traditions of Tibet. For Vajrayana practitioners, the most important among the five is the *Supreme Continuum*, which presents the classic view of buddha nature.

māra (Skt.; *bdud,* Tib.). The four māras are (1) the disturbing emotions *(kleśas),* (2) the five aggregates *(skandhas),* (3) the children of the gods *(devaputra),* and (4) death *(mṛtyupati)* or the Lord of Death (Yama). The Seventeenth Karmapa, Ogyen Trinley Dorjé, explains that in general, the label "māra" is given to what blocks a practitioner from attaining awakening or perfect liberation.

Marpa (*Mar pa lo tsā ba,* 1012–97). Known as Marpa the Translator for his prodigious work in bringing texts from India to Tibet. Among these were the teachings on mahāmudrā and Marpa's thirteen tantras, which form the core of practice in the Kagyü lineage. A married yogi, he was a student of Nāropa and teacher of Milarepa.

meditational deity. *See* yidam

Middle Way school (*madhyamaka,* Skt.; *dbu ma,* Tib.). The Middle Way school of philosophy evolved from the thought of the great Indian scholar Nāgārjuna. Its view focuses on the empty nature of all phenomena that allows for their dependent origination. Its reasonings radically cut through any tendency to reify an object or a subject. Of its two main subschools, the Rangtong approach emphasizes the empty aspect of mind's nature, while the Zhentong approach emphasizes its clear and radiant aspect. Ultimately, the two are inseparable.

Mikyö Dorjé, the Eighth Karmapa (*Mi bskyod rdo rje,* 1507–54). A prolific and profoundly learned scholar whose works include subtle commentaries on the major treatises of the Buddhist tradition and pithy instructions on the tantras. A great meditation master, he composed individual and group practice liturgies;

as a visionary artist, he developed the Karma Gardri *(Ka rma sgar bris)* style, one of the most important schools of thangka painting.

Milarepa *(Mi la ras pa,* 1040–1123). One of the main students of Marpa, he is famous as the poet yogi of Tibet. His spiritual songs cover the range of practice and experience, while his life story with all its hardships and ultimate success still inspires. Among his many realized disciples was Gampopa.

mother tantra *(ma rgyud,* Tib.). This form of tantric practice emphasizes wisdom. The generation stage practices focus on female deities, and the completion stage accentuates clear light.

mudrā (Skt.; *phya rgya,* Tib.). The term can mean "seal," "gesture," or "symbol." In Saraha's *A Song for the King,* it refers to the four seals.

Nāgārjuna (Skt.; *Klu sgrub,* Tib.). An Indian master who lived around the second century C.E. The Middle Way school bases its philosophy on his famous treatise elucidating emptiness, *The Fundamental Wisdom of the Middle Way.*

Nāropa (956–1040). A famous scholar turned siddha, Nāropa passed through twelve minor and twelve major hardships set by his teacher, Tilopa, and finally attained full awakening. He is renowned for creating the practice of six yogas and was the teacher of Marpa, who came from Tibet to study with him at Pullahari in India.

nirmāṇakāya. *See* kāyas

oral instructions *(upadeśa,* Skt.; *man ngag,* Tib.). Also translated as "key instructions," they are practical, pithy, and easily kept in mind. These teachings were often written down; nevertheless, they manage to maintain their original flavor of personal advice, derived from the experience of a master and given directly to the disciple.

passing experience *(nyams,* Tib.). In the mahāmudrā tradition, this refers to three types of temporary meditative experience—bliss, clarity, and nonthought—which appear as one practices along the path. They are indications that one has been meditating, but should not be allowed to fall into ego's domain or be grasped as real and solid.

path of liberation *(grol lam,* Tib.). This path emphasizes practices that work directly with the nature of mind. The term is paired with the path of method.

path of method (*thabs lam*, Tib.). This path emphasizes relative-level practices, such as the generation and completion stages and the six yogas of Nāropa. It should be practiced together with, and based upon, the path of liberation.

perfections (*pāramitā*, Skt.; *pha rol tu phyin pa*, Tib.). Also translated as "transcendent perfection," or more literally, "gone to the other shore," since by practicing them, one is carried across to the far shore of samsara and into liberation. As six, they are: generosity, discipline, patience, joyful diligence, stable contemplation, and deeper knowing or wisdom. As ten, four more are added: skillful means, aspiration, strength, and primordial wisdom. They constitute the bodhicitta of engagement and, along with meditation on the nature of the mind, form the path of a bodhisattva's practice.

prajñā (Skt.; *shes rab*, Tib.). A deeper knowing or wisdom that sees beyond the surface to a more profound reality, which can be seeing the impermanence of all phenomena or, more deeply, mind's nature itself. In dialectics, deeper knowing is traditionally defined as the faculty of the mind that is able to distinguish between relative and ultimate truths. *See* two truths

Prajñāpāramitā (Skt.; *shes rab kyi pha rol tu phyin pa*, Tib.). The term refers to the corpus of texts on emptiness and compassion that constitute the central teachings of the Mahayana. It also refers to the perfection *(pāramitā)* of wisdom *(prajñā)* and to the Great Mother, the embodiment of wisdom, who is considered the mother of all buddhas.

Rangjung Dorjé, the Third Karmapa (*Rang byung rdo rje*, 1284–1339). He studied all the teachings brought to Tibet, in particular the Nyingma Great Perfection tradition, which he united with the Kagyü mahāmudrā teachings. A prolific author, he wrote many influential treatises, among which the *Profound Inner Meaning* remains an important key to Vajrayana practice.

rūpakāya. *See* kāyas

sādhana (Skt; *sgrub thabs*, Tib.). A tantric practice for realizing the nature of a particular deity, who is the focus of the text. It usually begins with the preliminaries of taking refuge and generating bodhicitta, then moves to the main section of visualizing the deity and reciting its mantra, and closes with dissolution of the image and dedication.

samādhi (Skt.; *ting nge 'dzin*, Tib.). A meditative stabilization that involves undistracted, deep concentration when the practitioner's attention is exceptionally clear and focused one-pointedly. Many different kinds of samādhis are described in the sutras. In *A Song for the King,* four are emphasized: the samādhi of the lion's play (verse 30); the samādhi that realizes all appearances to be like an illusion (verse 31); the samādhi of the hero's stride (verse 32); and the vajralike samādhi (verse 33).

śamatha (Skt.; *gzhi gnas,* Tib.). Common to most Buddhist schools, this is a meditation practice of bringing one's mind into sustained tranquility. The Tibetan literally means "calm abiding." Through repeated practice, distractions are stilled and the mind is able to abide wherever it is placed. Calm abiding is the basis for the practice of vipaśyanā, or deeper insight.

sambhogakāya. *See* kāyas

samsara (*saṃsāra,* Skt.; *'khor ba,* Tib.). Also translated as "cyclic existence," where, due to basic ignorance, one circulates birth after birth through the three realms (desire, form, and formless) or through the six types of rebirth (as a hell being, hungry ghost, animal, human, demigod, or god). Birth, old age, sickness, and death are the forms of suffering particular to human birth; all types of suffering are transcended when the nature of mind is fully realized.

secret mantra (*gsang ngag,* Tib.). A synonym for the Vajrayana.

siddha (Skt.; *grub thob,* Tib.). "One who has attained accomplishment," or an enlightened master in the Vajrayana tradition. The eighty-four mahāsiddhas ("great masters"), including Saraha, Tilopa, and Nāropa, were Indian adepts who followed very diverse lifestyles both while attaining realization and subsequently in their teaching methods.

siddhi (Skt.; *dngos grub,* Tib.). Usually translated as "accomplishments," they are divided into ordinary or supreme. The ordinary siddhis refer to mundane powers such as clairvoyance, and the supreme siddhi is complete and full enlightenment.

six yogas of Nāropa (*Na ro chos drug,* Tib.). They belong to the path of method and consist of four major practices: (1) inner heat *(gtum mo);* (2) illusory body *(sgyu lus);* (3) dream yoga *(rmi lam);* and (4) clear light *('od gsal).* The two adjunct practices are (5) transference of consciousness *('pho ba)* and (6) the intermediate state *(bar do).*

skillful means (*upāya,* Skt.; *thabs,* Tib.). Meditation practice has two wings: skillful means and wisdom or, respectively, compassion and emptiness. Skillful means refers to compassionate activity and the great variety of ways to train in it.

sugatagarbha (Skt.). The Tibetan, *bde gshegs snying po,* literally means "the heart essence of the One Gone to Bliss." It is also translated as buddha nature.

superimposition (*sgro 'dogs,* Tib.). Literally, "to attach feathers." The term means to assume that something exists that does not, for example, a permanent and autonomous self. The term is also translated as "conceptual overlay," "exaggeration," and "overestimation." *See also* denial

sutra (*sūtra,* Skt.; *mdo,* Tib.). Refers to the second of the three sections (the Vinaya, Sūtra, and Abhidharma) of the tripiṭaka, the early compilation of Śākyamuni Buddha's teachings. More generally, a sutra is a text containing the discourses of Śākyamuni Buddha or those inspired by him. Sutras are often in the form of a dialogue between the Buddha and a disciple concerning a particular topic. Within discussions of philosophical view, the sutra approach refers to a gradual path to enlightenment, as distinguished from the swift path of the Vajrayana.

svābhāvikakāya. *See* kāyas

tantra (Skt.; *rgyud,* Tib.). Usually translated as "continuum" or "thread," the term refers to the esoteric teachings and practices given by the Buddha in his sambhogakāya form. Tantra is synonymous with the Vajrayana and can also refer to a text that presents these teachings or practices. The translation "continuum" points to the continuity of mind's nature in the beginning as the ground, in the middle along the path as it is being discovered, and at the end when it fully manifests as the fruition.

three vehicles (*triyāna,* Skt; *theg pa gsum,* Tib.). These refer to the three paths taken by three types of practitioner: the hearer (*śrāvaka,* Skt.), the solitary sage (*pratyekabuddha,* Skt.), and the bodhisattva. According to Mahayana teachings, practitioners belonging to the first two vehicles of the hearers and solitary sages will eventually enter the path of the bodhisattva and thereby attain complete and full awakening. In English, the three vehicles also refer to the Hinayana, the Mahayana, and Vajrayana.

Tilopa (988–1069). Indian mahāsiddha who received the teachings directly from Vajradhara and became the first lineage holder of the Kagyü tradition. Tilopa passed these teachings to Nāropa, who transmitted them to Marpa, who in turn gave them to Milarepa. Tilopa is known for attaining mahāmudrā realization while pounding sesame seeds and for his doha, "The River Ganges Mahāmudrā."

twelve deeds of the Buddha (*mdzad pa bcu gnyis,* Tib.). Though Buddhas are considered already enlightened, they perform twelve deeds for the sake of their disciples: (1) descending from the heaven of Tuṣita where he had resided; (2) entering the womb of his mother, Māyadevi; (3) taking birth; (4) becoming skilled in worldly arts and demonstrating physical prowess; (5) taking pleasure in the retinue of his queen and consorts; (6) turning away from the world; (7) practicing asceticism; (8) going to take his vajra seat under the Bodhi tree; (9) conquering the māras; (10) becoming fully awakened; (11) turning the wheel of the Dharma teachings; and (12) passing into nirvāṇa.

twelve links of dependent origination (*pratītyasamutpāda,* Skt.; *rten 'brel bcu gnyis,* Tib.). In general, these are the stages passed through as we cycle in samsara; they can also refer to other processes, such as the arising of a thought: (1) ignorance, (2) karmic impulses, (3) consciousness, (4) name and form, (5) the six sources of consciousness, (6) contact, (7) feeling, (8) craving, (9) grasping, (10) becoming, (11) birth, and (12) old age and death.

two truths (*dvisatya,* Skt.; *bden pa gnyis,* Tib.). The relative truth and the ultimate truth are two levels of perception; one is dualistic and the other, beyond duality. Relative truth involves experience in terms of a subject and object; it is what appears to the confused mind of an ordinary being. Ultimate truth transcends duality; it is a synonym for emptiness and clarity inseparable that appears to those who have realized mind's true nature.

Vajradhara (Skt.; *rdo rje 'chang,* Tib.). Within the Vajrayana, this is a synonym for the complete realization of mind's nature. In general, Vajradhara is the name of the dharmakāya buddha, who is dark blue in color and holds a bell and vajra. He is important for the Kagyü lineage, as Tilopa is said to have received the Vajrayana teachings directly from him.

Vajrayana (*vajrayāna,* Skt.; *rdo rje theg pa,* Tib.). It is said that like a diamond, a vajra is able to cut through everything, and this quality makes it a symbol for the realization of mind's nature that cuts through all delusions of duality.

Yāna means "vehicle" and so the term is often translated as "diamond vehicle," a synonym for the tantric Buddhism that developed in India and came to Tibet, forming the core of its Buddhist practice.

Vajrayoginī (Skt.; *rdo rje rnal 'byor ma,* Tib.). Embodying wisdom, she is a major form of female deity practice in the Kagyü lineage. Red in color, she stands in a dancing posture. Vajravārāhī is based on a similar deity.

valid cognition (*pramāṇa,* Skt.; *tshad ma,* Tib). Traditionally, there are three types. Direct valid cognition refers to nonconceptual, unmistaken perception by the five sense faculties, by the mental faculty, by self-awareness, and by yogic experience. Inferential valid cognition refers to classes of valid proofs or reasonings that lead to a developed understanding of mind's nature. Scriptural valid cognition refers to texts that are the authentic word of the Buddha.

vipaśyanā (Skt.; *lhag mthong,* Tib.). Often translated as "insight meditation" or "deeper insight." Coming after the mind has been stabilized through the practice of śamatha, deep insight involves seeing into the nature of mind itself.

Wangchuk Dorjé, the Ninth Karmapa (*Dbang phyug rdo rje,* 1556–1603). He is renowned for his three treatises on mahāmudrā: *The Ocean of Definitive Meaning* (the most extensive), *Eliminating the Darkness of Ignorance* (much shorter), and *Pointing Out the Dharmakāya* (a condensation of the core practices).

yidam (Tib.). The fully awakened mind manifesting as the different forms of deities who represent its myriad qualities. Often translated as "chosen deity," it refers to the specific deity selected as the focus of one's practice. The yidam is known as the root of accomplishments, or siddhis.

Bibliography

Tibetan Works

Dbang phyug rdor rje, Rgyal dbang Ka rma pa, *Lhan cig skyes sbyor gyi zab khrid nges don rgya mtsho'i snying po phrin las 'od 'phro.* Rumtek, Sikkim: Dharma Chakra Centre, n.d.

Karma chags med. *'Phags pa thugs rje chen po'i dmar khrid phyag rdzogs zung 'jugs gi nyams len snying po bsdus pa.* From *Gdam ngag mdzod,* vol. Ta., ff. 1–12 (roman 325–47). Delhi: Sechen Publications, 1999.

Karma 'phrin las pa. *Do ha skor gsum ti ka 'bring po sems kyi rnam thar ston pa'i me long.* Kunzang Tobgyel, Thimphu, Bhutan: Druk Sherig Press, 1984.

———. *Rgyal po do ha'i ti ka 'bring po sems kyi rnam thar ston pa'i me long* in *Do ha skor gsum ti ka 'bring po sems kyi rnam thar ston pa'i me long* (roman 159–215). Published by Kunzang Tobgyel, Thimphu, Bhutan: Druk Sherig Press, 1984.

Smen sdong mtsham pa. *Byams smon 'grel chung byang chub bde lam. (The Prayer of Maitreya and An Easy Path to Enlightenment: A Short Commentary on the Aspiration Prayer of Maitreya.)* Translated by Michele Martin. Kathmandu: Marpa Institute for Translators, 1996.

Saraha. *Dohakoshagiti. Do ha mdzod gyi glu.* Delhi: *sDe-dge Bstan-'gyur.* Delhi Karmapae Chodhey Gyalwae Sungrab Partun Khang, 1982–1985, *Rgyud 'grel* (D2224), vol. Wi., ff. 70b–77a. (Referred to as *A Song for the People.*)

———. *Dohakoshanamacaryagiti. Do ha mdzod ces bya ba spyod pa'i glu.* Delhi: *sDe-dge Bstan-'gyur.* Delhi Karmapae Chodhey Gyalwae Sungrab Partun Khang, 1982–1985, *Rgyud 'grel* (D2263), vol. Zhi, ff. 26b–28b. (Referred to as *A Song for the King.*) The Tibetan Buddhist Resource Center holds digitally scanned images of this text. See www.tbrc.org and number W23703.

English-Language Works

Conze, Edward, ed. *Buddhist Wisdom.* New York: Vintage Spiritual Books, 2001. (Translations and commentaries of the *Diamond Sutra* and *Heart Sutra.*)

Davidson, Ronald M. *Indian Esoteric Buddhism: A Social History of the Tantric Movement.* New York: Columbia University Press, 2002.

Guenther, Herbert V., tr. *Ecstatic Spontaneity: Saraha's Three Cycles of Doha.* Fremont, CA: Asian Humanities Press, 1993.

———. *The Royal Song of Saraha: A Study in the History of Buddhist Thought.* Seattle: University of Washington Press, 1969. Reprint, Taipei: SMC Publishing, 1992.

Gyatso, Janet, ed. *In the Mirror of Memory: Reflections on Mindfulness and Remembrance in Indian and Tibetan Buddhism.* Albany: State University of New York Press, 1992.

Jackson, Roger. *Tantric Treasures: Three Collections of Mystical Verses from Buddhist India.* New York: Oxford University Press, 2004.

Linrothe, Rob. *Holy Madness: Portraits of Tantric Siddhas.* Chicago: Serinidia, 2006.

Nālandā Translation Committee, tr. *The Rain of Wisdom: The Essence of the Ocean of True Meaning.* Boston: Shambhala Publications, 1989.

Namgyal, Dakpo Tashi. *Clarifying the Natural State.* Translated by Erik Pema Kunsang. Boudanath: Rangjung Yeshe Publications, 2001.

———. *Mahamudra: The Quintessence of Mind and Meditation.* Translated by Lobsang P. Lhalungpa. Boston: Shambhala Publications, 1986. Revised edition, Boston: Wisdom Publications, 2006.

Roerich, George N. *The Blue Annals.* Delhi: Motilal Banarsidass, 1949, 1976.

Ruegg, David Seyfort. *Buddha-Nature, Mind and the Problem of Gradualism in a Comparative Perspective: On the Transmission and Reception of Buddhism in India and Tibet.* New Delhi: Heritage Publishers, 1992.

Schaeffer, Kurtis R. *Dreaming the Great Brahmin: Tibetan Traditions of the Buddhist Poet-Saint Saraha.* New York: Oxford University Press, 2005.

Thrangu Rinpoche, Khenchen. *Essentials of Mahamudra: Looking Directly at the Mind.* Boston: Wisdom Publications, 2004.

———. *The Ninth Karmapa's "Ocean of Definitive Meaning."* Ithaca, NY: Snow Lion Publications, 2003.

———. *An Ocean of the Ultimate Meaning: Teachings on Mahamudra.* Translated by Peter Alan Roberts. Boston: Shambhala Publications, 2004.

———. *The Ornament of Clear Realization: A Commentary on the Prajnaparamita by Maitreya.* Crestone, CO: Namo Buddha Publications; and Auckland, New Zealand: Zhyisil Chokyi Ghatsal Charitable Trust Publications, 2004.

————. *Pointing Out the Dharmakaya.* Ithaca, NY: Snow Lion Publications, 2003.

Waddell, Norman, tr. *Zen Words for the Heart: Hakuin's Commentary on the Heart Sutra.* Boston: Shambhala Publications, 1996.

Wangchuk Dorjé, the Ninth Gyalwang Karmapa. *Mahamudra: The Ocean of Definitive Meaning.* Translated by Elizabeth M. Callahan. Seattle: Nitartha International, 2001.

A Brief Biography of Thrangu Rinpoche

THRANGU RINPOCHE was born in Kham, Tibet, in 1933 and was recognized at age five as the incarnation of the previous Thrangu Tulku by the Sixteenth Karmapa and the Eleventh Situ Rinpoche. Entering Thrangu Monastery as a young boy, he studied reading, writing, grammar, poetry, and astrology, memorized ritual texts, and completed two preliminary retreats. At sixteen he began the study of the three vehicles of Buddhism while staying in retreat and received full ordination from the Karmapa at twenty-three.

In 1959 Thrangu Rinpoche left Tibet for India at the time of the Chinese military takeover. At thirty-five he took the geshe examination before 1,500 monks in India and was awarded the degree of Geshe Lharampa, the highest degree granted in the Gelugpa tradition. Subsequently he was named abbot of Rumtek Monastery, the Karmapa's seat in Sikkim, India, and became the personal teacher of the four principal Karma Kagyü tulkus.

For years Thrangu Rinpoche has traveled and taught extensively, establishing centers in Europe, Asia, and North America. He is also the abbot of Gampo Abbey in Nova Scotia, Canada. Rinpoche's educational institutions in Nepal include a monastery, Thrangu Tashi Chöling; a retreat center and monastic college at Namo Buddha; a school for the general education of lay children and young monks; and Thrangu Tara Abbey, which offers a full Dharma education for nuns. Vajra Vidya Institute, a beautiful monastic college in Sarnath, India, the site of the Buddha's first teaching, opened in 1999. Most recently, Rinpoche has established a retreat center for his Western students in Crestone, Colorado. In 2000 Thrangu Rinpoche was appointed the personal tutor of the Seventeenth Karmapa, Ogyen Trinley Dorjé.

For more information about Thrangu Rinpoche and his activities, contact his website: www.rinpoche.com

About the Translators

MICHELE MARTIN has been a Buddhist practitioner for over thirty years. After receiving graduate degrees from Yale, she studied in Japan, India, and Nepal with masters of meditation and scholars, while also serving as an oral translator and editing Buddhist books. Her publications include *Music in the Sky: The Life, Art, and Teachings of the 17th Karmapa Ogyen Trinley Dorje* and translations from Tibetan texts on philosophy and meditation. She lives in the Catskill Mountains of upstate New York.

PETER O'HEARN (Lama Yeshe Gyamtso) has completed two three-year retreats under the guidance of Kalu Rinpoche and is one of the most respected translators of the Kagyü lineage. He is a translator at Karma Triyana Dharmachakra, the seat of the Gyalwang Karmapa in the West, and travels widely as a translator for the main Kagyü lamas. Among his published work are *The Instructions of Gampopa* and *Precious Essence: The Inner Autobiography of Terchen Barway Dorje*. He lives with his wife and daughter in the Hudson Valley.

About Wisdom Publications

Wisdom Publications, a nonprofit publisher, is dedicated to making available authentic Buddhist works for the benefit of all. We publish translations of the sutras and tantras, commentaries and teachings of past and contemporary Buddhist masters, and original works by the world's leading Buddhist scholars. We publish our titles with the appreciation of Buddhism as a living philosophy and with the special commitment to preserve and transmit important works from all the major Buddhist traditions.

If you would like more information or a copy of our mail order catalog, please write or call us at this address:

Wisdom Publications
199 Elm Street
Somerville, Massachusetts, 02144 USA
Tel: (617) 776-7416 • Fax: (617) 776-7841
www.wisdompubs.org • info@wisdompubs.org

The Wisdom Trust

As a nonprofit publisher, Wisdom Publications is dedicated to the publication of fine Dharma books for the benefit of all sentient beings and dependent upon the kindness and generosity of sponsors in order to do so. If you would like to make a donation to Wisdom please contact our Somerville office.

Thank you.

Wisdom Publications is a nonprofit, charitable 501(c)(3) organization and a part of the Foundation for the Preservation of the Mahayana Tradition (FPMT).